WEB 2.0 AND BEYOND

WEB 2.0 AND BEYOND

Understanding the New Online
Business Models, Trends,
and Technologies

Tom Funk

PRAEGER

Westport, Connecticut
London

Library of Congress Cataloging-in-Publication Data

Funk, Tom, 1965–
Web 2.0 and beyond : understanding the new online business models, trends, and technologies / Tom Funk.
    p.   cm.
  Includes bibliographical references and index.
  ISBN 978-0-313-35187-7 (alk. paper)
    1. Electronic commerce.   2. Web 2.0.   3. Internet marketing.
4. Information technology—Management.   I. Title.
  HF5548.32.F863   2009
  658.8′72—dc22   2008020074

British Library Cataloguing in Publication Data is available.

Library of Congress Catalog Card Number: 2008020074
ISBN 978-0-313-35187-7

First published in 2009

Praeger Publishers, 88 Post Road West, Westport, CT 06881
An imprint of Greenwood Publishing Group, Inc.
www.praeger.com

Printed in the United States of America

The paper used in this book complies with the Permanent Paper Standard issued by the National Information Standards Organization (Z39.48–1984).

10 9 8 7 6 5 4 3 2

To my wife Elizabeth, and to the Funks 2.0: Hannah, Molly, and Louisa

Contents

Acknowledgments

I would like to thank my editor, Jeff Olson, and Greenwood Publishing Group for developing the idea for this book and shepherding it to completion. Thanks to my wonderful and supportive wife Elizabeth, and daughters Hannah, Molly, and Louisa, who bore with me many months after I was sure I'd be finished with the project! Thanks to Seth Godin, Lauren Freedman, Phil Wainewright, and others who were generous with their time and considerable insights by granting me interviews. Thanks to Bud Reed and the rest of the Timberline Interactive team, who afforded me the speaking and conference-hopping schedule (and the few groggy mornings after late-night writing stints), which helped bring this book to fruition. Thanks to the writers in my life, especially Don Mitchell and my mother Donna Lee, who inspired me by example. Thanks to Timberline clients, and colleagues at other companies, who continually share experiences and know-how, and provide me a constant source of education and energy. Thanks to Internet Retailer, the DMA, Vermont/New Hampshire Direct Marketing Group, and others for granting me speaking platforms.

Finally, I thank the reader—and I hope these pages help you approach Web 2.0 not with intimidation, but with inspiration!

Introduction: What is Web 2.0 and How Will It Change My Business?

"Web 2.0" has taken on buzzword status. It's being applied as shorthand for everything that is new, cutting-edge, and gaining momentum online. Web 2.0 can describe particular websites, cultural trends like social networking, blogging or podcasting, or the underlying technology and rich, streaming media that makes today's coolest web applications possible.

As with any buzzword, the hype can be a tad overdone. For one thing, Web 2.0 isn't especially new. But today, many of its technologies and best practices have moved within the reach and budget of any online business. What are the major themes of Web 2.0?

- Power is in the hands of individual users and their networks.
- Web content is distributed, sorted, combined, and displayed across the web in formats unanticipated by the content creators.
- New technology now makes rich online experiences and complex software applications possible.
- Integration is breaking down walls between PCs, phones and mobile devices, marketing and ordering channels, and a user's experience across different websites.

With examples from real businesses, this book demonstrates how any company can adopt Web 2.0 approaches, regardless of its size or resources. The book is a nontechnical guide, aimed at the marketer or business manager who wants to understand recent developments in the online world, and to turn them to practical advantage in his or her own organization. If there's an area you would like to pursue, you needn't go it alone. There's an army of consultants and web development firms ready to help you.

Web 2.0 is a landscape where users control their online experience and influence the experiences of others; where success comes from harnessing the power of social networks, computing networks, media and opinion networks, and advertising networks.

In Web 2.0, your company's profile within these interlinked networks increasingly determines how your brand is perceived—and even where your website ranks in the search engines.

Web 2.0 takes advantage of higher bandwidth and lighter-weight programming tools to create rich, engaging, online experiences that compete with television and other offline activities. Web 2.0 offers powerful applications not as packaged software but on demand across the internet. Web 2.0 is just beginning to integrate the flood of tools, data, and hardware in your life: your contacts, calendar, and messaging, your PC and your PDA, those countless usernames and passwords, your income tax filing, bank, and brokerage account.

█ "Honey, I'm Home!"

When we think too much about the technologies driving these trends, or the dollars involved, it's time to step back and recognize that above all, Web 2.0 is a uniquely human, cultural event.

What is special about the web right now are the networks of people emotionally and creatively engaged with the internet and with each other. Whether they are chatting, dancing, or doing business with other players in a 3-D virtual world like Second Life, or producing and uploading their own podcast, or researching a health issue on a special interest forum, today's users are more intensely engaged with the web than ever before.

How engaged are they? Enough that they don't miss having a sweetheart.

Nearly one in four Americans say that the internet can serve as a substitute for a significant other for some period of time, according to a poll released in December 2007 by 463 Communications and Zogby International.

The Zogby/463 Internet Attitudes poll found that 24% of Americans said the internet could serve as a replacement for a significant other. Among singles, the figure is 31%.

That may sound depressing. Certainly the web has its share of creepy and depressed denizens, addicted to porn, gambling, or some other vice, or frittering away hours indulging in an avatar-based fantasy life, while neglecting their *real* life. But much of what is best about Web 2.0 reflects well on our humanity and social nature. The richness and interactivity of Web 2.0, the availability of video, audio, webcam, VOIP (Voice Over Internet Protocol, also known as "internet telephony"), and live chat, the opportunity for creative expression in words and images, and the energetic bazaar of social network sites make today's web a dynamic, personal, and rewarding experience. That's why the hours we spend on the web have eaten into so many other leisure time activities, and why so many have come to see it as a replacement for a mate.

Increasingly, one's online life *is* real life.

▒ Remembering the Early Web

The term Web 2.0 has been applied so broadly—to programming tools, social networking behavior, high-bandwidth rich media, marketing tactics, and more—it may be more useful to think in terms of what Web 2.0 is *not*. In other words, what was the World Wide Web like in its early years?

The internet has been around since 1969, when the U.S. military's Defense Advanced Research Projects Agency (DARPA) and its university and contactor partners first strung together four networked computers into what was then known as ARPANET. For the better part of two decades the internet remained the province of academics and government, until emerging into the consciousness of early adopters with the two early internet service providers to gain wide consumer use, Compuserve and then AmericaOnline.

In the 1980s, the consumer usefulness of the internet was still little more than text-only bulletin-boards and newsgroups, plus the beginnings of electronic mail. It was exciting for techies and early adopters, but pretty dry stuff to the average consumer or businessperson. From a consumer and pop-culture perspective, the worldwide network of computers was a solution waiting for a problem.

The introduction in 1991 by Tim Berners-Lee of the World Wide Web changed everything. The invention of the Web laid the foundation of interlinked (or "hyperlinked") documents containing text and graphics viewable in a new software application called the web browser.

The early web was for the most part a collection of "pages" of static information, updated and uploaded by hand. Low-bandwidth modem connections kept image sizes to a minimum, and the medium gravitated toward simple displays of text and smallish graphics. But despite its handicaps, the commercial web revolutionized communication and commerce with the promise of millions of connected people, businesses, and organizations worldwide—and of digital stores that could expand indefinitely without incremental costs.

Soon came the rapid hockey stick we know as the internet bubble, a period of rapid user adoption, breathless media attention, extravagant business plans, and absurd stock valuations.

I built my first website in 1995, for an antique and classic car collectibles business called *Mobilia*. The site was constructed utterly by hand in HTML, and was utterly static: New content was authored manually and uploaded to the servers piecemeal every day.

A few frenzied years went by, interest in the internet heated up, and the site was upgraded: It was no longer a collection of static pages, but (like virtually all websites today) a software application that assembled web pages dynamically by reaching into a database of products, articles, news stories, images, customers, etc. Like so many companies in the bubble era, we attracted a few million dollars of venture capital money, built a more ambitious ecommerce platform—and then ran out of money.

By 2000, the air was rapidly going out of the bubble. I moved to the Vermont Teddy Bear Company as web manager, and Mobilia soon shut its doors.

At Vermont Teddy Bear I saw a different perspective on ecommerce: frugal, customer-focused, built on direct-response financial realities, and dependably profitable. By the time I left VTB in 2007, the company was doing about $52 million in business on the web, at peak holiday seasons transacting up to 2,000 orders an hour.

Today, at the web development and online marketing firm Timberline Interactive, we work with a broad spectrum of businesses: travel and tourism operations, gift companies, apparel sellers, merchants in the food, gardening, and education fields. Among our clients are King Arthur Flour, Garrett Wade tool company, VBT Bicycling Vacations, Yarn.com, American Meadows, Gorton's Fresh Seafood, Dinn Brothers Trophies, and the Lake Champlain Chocolate Company.

What I've learned working with these companies, and from my fellow ecommerce managers, is that to succeed online you need to keep one eye on the new trends and technologies that everyone's buzzing about—and one eye on the established basics *no one* is buzzing about anymore, but which are still as important as ever. So it is with Web 2.0. Part of our job is educating ourselves about the new landscape, and separating fact from hype. Then we can identify promising opportunities worthy of our time and money, and pick a few more speculative areas for tire-kicking.

This book doesn't make any attempt to chronicle the launches and buy-outs that are such a huge part of the daily scramble between companies for prominence in the Web 2.0 world. Speculating on Google owning a swath of the wireless spectrum, Microsoft acquiring Yahoo!—all the big players maneuvering to snap up innovative little advertising platforms, vertical search engines, and social networks—that's the province of the news and tech media. We will concern ourselves with best practices to help you participate in Web 2.0's social and business trends, and effectively use the technology that enables them.

▦ What Is Web 2.0?

Web 2.0 describes the upgraded, improved, and modernized World Wide Web we're using today. It's a term used loosely to apply to everything from the explosion of social networking websites like MySpace and YouTube, to the rich, interactive software applications being served online, and even to the specific programming languages and technology tools that make the "new" web possible.

Web 2.0 is a social transformation that has put more interactivity and control of content into the hands of regular users, not just big site own-ers. It's faster and more interactive than Web 1.0. Increased bandwidth, always-on connections, and higher speeds mean that rich media con-tent like Flash and streaming video, webcasts, podcasts, streaming au-dio, software, music and video downloads, and multiplayer role-playing games have become a regular part of the online experience, letting the web take its place at the table alongside traditional entertainment media.

The two people most associated with popularizing the term Web 2.0, John Battelle and Tim O'Reilly, gave it a very broad definition. I won't hew exactly to their outline, preferring to delve a bit deeper into social and marketing aspects of Web 2.0, and away from technology. But I'll try to summarize (and paraphrase) the Web 2.0 hallmarks Battelle and O'Reilly identified.[1]

- The Web as Platform
  The internet is an interactive computer application, not just a network.
- Harnessing Collective Intelligence
  With online collaboration like wikis and open-source development, the whole is greater than the sum of its parts.

- Data Is the Next "Intel Inside"
  The quality and open availability of data is what matters—not its particular format or where it's found.
- End of the Software Release Cycle
  When applications are served across the web as a service, upgrades are made rapidly and constantly.
- Lightweight Programming Models
  New scripting languages and file formats make for faster, more interactive websites—sites that interact with users and with other sites and data sources.
- Rich User Experiences
  The web is a more dynamic and entertaining place, thanks to high bandwidth connections, streaming video, audio, and animation.
- Software above the Level of a Single Device
  The web extends not only to PCs but also to PDAs, cell phones, and other mobile devices.

Clearly, this conception of Web 2.0 is a broad one—one well-suited to the scope of the revolutionary changes that have been happening online. But it's also a definition that is vulnerable to a great deal of stretching.

Writing in *eWeek*, the computer and internet journalist, John Pallatto, said of Web 2.0, "The problem is that the term, perhaps like all good marketing terms, is as malleable as kids' modeling clay. Anybody doing business on the web can claim that they are adherents of the Web 2.0 movement."[2]

Indeed, some jaded folks in the industry now deride the latest, over-hyped little social networking site or widget by labeling it YAW2.0 ("Yet Another Web 2.0") or YASN (Yet Another Social Network).

"AJAX, Ruby on Rails, RSS, wikis or any other reputed Web 2.0 technology won't make any business successful unless they are built into web applications that work, are useful, make money and deliver value to customers," says Pallatto. "Every venture, no matter what technology it uses, has to be judged on its own merits, not because it carries some catchy label."

░ Who Coined the Term "Web 2.0"?

People have been talking about Web 2.0 since not long after the first wave of commercial internet peaked and crashed in March 2000. As I said, credit for popularizing the term usually goes to web visionaries and publishing execs Tim O'Reilly and John Battelle.

In 2004, O'Reilly, founder and CEO of computer book publisher O'Reilly Media, and John Battelle, founder of *The Industry Standard* and an original editor of *Wired* magazine and HotWired.com, launched their ground-breaking Web 2.0 Conference in San Francisco to spotlight emerging technologies and innovation on the web.

Today the conference, organized by CMP Media and produced by Media-Live International, goes by the name Web 2.0 Summit. CMP holds a U.S. trademark for the term "Web 2.0" when applied to trade shows, conferences, and events.

The concept of "Web 2.0" began with a conference brainstorming session between O'Reilly Media and MediaLive International. It was later described in fuller detail in an article written by Tim O'Reilly in *What Is Web 2.0: Design Patterns and Business Models for the Next Generation of Software* on September 30, 2005.

Although Battelle and O'Reilly are the names most associated with Web 2.0, it was two years earlier, in 2002 (when the dust was rising from the dotcom bust) that Dermot McCormack published the book, *Web 2.0: The Resurgence of the Internet and eCommerce.*

Even if they weren't its inventors, Battelle and O'Reilly are certainly Web 2.0's Henry Ford: They defined it for a popular audience, and redefine its leading edge each year with their Web 2.0 Summit.

O'Reilly sums up his vision of Web 2.0 like this: "Web 2.0 doesn't have a hard boundary, but rather, a gravitational core. You can visualize Web 2.0 as a set of principles and practices that tie together a veritable solar system of sites that demonstrate some or all of those principles, at a varying distance from that core."

▓ Innovations within Reach of Any Budget

At this writing, the most visited websites are dominated by Web 2.0 poster children. Among the top are the search and portal giants Yahoo!, Google, and MSN (which are all actively rolling out many Web 2.0 innovations), plus the leading ecommerce properties, Amazon and eBay. The remaining five are all Web 2.0 phenomena:

- Social networks MySpace and Facebook
- Streaming video network YouTube
- Software-as-a-Service platforms Windows Live, Gmail, and Yahoo Mail
- Wikipedia

But just because Web 2.0 sites are among the biggest, most popular sites today doesn't mean they require massive scale, cutting-edge developers, and huge budgets to participate in the same trends. Many Web 2.0 innovations were pioneered by behemoths like Google, Amazon, Apple, YouTube, and MySpace—but today you can leverage some of the same benefits on a shoestring budget. Even the smallest, leanest companies can take advantage of the new trends, new and open-source programming tools, and new networks. This book will present ideas for any business to quickly and affordably deploy Web 2.0 best practices.

Throughout this book I'll point to leading examples of Web 2.0 technologies and practices—but I'll also attempt to reel it back into relevance to the average small to medium-sized enterprise wanting to stay current without making huge bets against unproven odds. Thankfully, by the very nature of Web 2.0, many of the most attractive trends are the most open, the most democratic, and the easiest for you to participate in without making big technology investments. Lots of brilliant, creative minds have been developing new technologies you can now join without breaking the bank.

As we'll see in the coming chapters, when you put Web 2.0 design principles to work in your business, you'll create:

- Stronger, more personalized connections with your customers.
- Positive, brand-building connections among customers.
- Feedback loops enabling you to test and improve your website's performance based on customer behavior.
- A clearer focus on the unique value of your product, services, information, or data—regardless of how it's displayed or where it appears.
- Strategies for integrating your website with other devices and channels.
- A website that is truly an interactive tool for serving your customer.

1 ▪ ▪ ▪

Power to the People

Marketers and business managers can easily fall into the trap of thinking it's all about them. After all, they pour the blood, sweat, and tears into their products or services. They sit in endless meetings about brand image, their marketing plan, their website's look and feel, and how it functions.

But of course, it's all about consumers, and whether your product or service suits their needs, solves their problems, and does it in a special, innovative, or remarkable way. And today's web is better than ever at putting power into the consumers' hands.

Today's consumers are not passive receivers of your advertising messages. They are increasingly sophisticated and skeptical, and increasingly active in seeking out the information, opinions, products, and services that interest them. The web is one of the principal ways they do so.

The web is trillions of pages on a couple of hundred million websites, viewed by 1.25 billion people. They hail from every country and walk of life, and increasingly they don't merely visit: They link to, comment upon, and modify what they see. Using Web 2.0 tools they "tag" pictures, blog posts, articles, and web pages with key words and phrases that help other users find, sort, and classify online material. Increasingly, they can modify their own personal pages and portals to add customized content, from local weather forecasts and stock portfolios to tiny, portable programs called "widgets." Their interaction with the web changes it every moment. Interactivity is probably the single most important attribute of Web 2.0.

Even referring to the web as "pages" is a misnomer. While initially many pages served on the internet were static files, today what you view in your web browser, or the screen of your phone or PDA, or receive as an alert in your email client, is data—information served up dynamically, shaped to your particular request and personal identity.

People using the web and publishing on it today have the power to create new content, effortlessly launch new websites, and make blog posts or comments. Call it the "social web," or the "participatory web."

Not only is the shape of the information fluid, but so is your company's operating environment and even its reputation. Your customers and prospects will experience your content the way they prefer, pass it around, reformat it, and comment on it. In the process they shape opinions about your organization and your products.

They may help your search-engine visibility, and they may perform promotional efforts on your behalf. They may embarrass you in public.

Today, successful companies are embracing the power of the people and using it to enhance everything they do online.

▓ Interactivity, Then and Now

Interactivity between people has always been a central part of the commercial internet. The first popular online activities were all about communication: Usenet forums, Compuserv chat rooms, email. Individual people connecting on whatever topic interested them predated the brochureware—static web pages—and online stores of the early web. User-driven communication lost the spotlight to big ecommerce sites and portals for a few years, but it has all come back again to people.

What is new about Web 2.0 interactivity is that it now goes so far beyond messaging. It's not just about people interacting with other people. It's people modifying websites in the process of interacting with other people: posting text commentary and opinions; uploading and tagging photos, creating videos, audio streams, online conferencing, and collaboration; and visiting the 3-D virtual worlds of multiplayer online games.

Web 2.0 programming tools and cultural trends have produced an explosion of new forms of websites. Blogs were the first personal web publishing phenomenon. But now the legions of vibrant, interconnected blogs have been joined by a host of other types of instant websites. Wikis, social networks, and basic online stores can all now be launched inexpensively and quickly, by almost anyone.

Meanwhile, the websites of the world's businesses and organizations are becoming ever more interactive. Features pioneered by Amazon.com and others a decade ago have now become "best practices" and are available in some form on most web platforms and in third-party software tools. Comments, user profile pages, product reviews and ratings—user-created pages are sprouting like flowers. *Social media* or social networking sites like YouTube, MySpace, Facebook, Flickr, Digg, LinkedIn, and others have experienced viral growth, by pairing a popular activity (music, video, photo sharing, business) with the network effect inherent in "friend" sites.

Let's first look at a number of online developments that are putting power into the hands of ordinary web users:

- Blogs
- Social Networks
- Wikis and Online Collaboration
- Tagging
- User-Submitted Reviews and Ratings
- New Online Authorities
- Instant Websites
- Mashups
- Widgets

The Blogosphere

Blogs are no longer front-page news, but now that the dust has settled, it's clearer to see the remarkable impacts of the blogging phenomenon, and to separate them from the hype.

Blogs (a contraction of "weblog," an online diary of sorts) have been around in some form since the 1990s. The Open Diary blog platform launched in 1998, and Blogger in 1999.

By election year 2004, American media had latched onto blogging as symbolic of the democratization of the web: Web content was no longer the sole province of the big portals and media companies. Millions of ordinary people could create websites and publish information quickly, cheaply, and without technical know-how. Blogs like the Drudge report, Instapundit, and Wonkette could scoop the mainstream media. By 2006, *Time* magazine pointed to blogging and other user-created web content in its celebration of the Person of the Year as "You."

Fast forward to the current day, and blogs are so accepted a part of the conversation that mainstream reporters routinely contact industry and pundit bloggers, tapping them as experts for sound bites for their articles.

Blogs are a crucial element of the Web 2.0 landscape not just for the information they publish, but for the spider web of relationships they spawn: relationships among blogs, between authors and their sources of inspiration, and between authors and their community of readers. All these relationships are expressed by hyperlinks.

The culture of the blogosphere is one of linking to and commenting upon posts, displaying "trackback" links (one blogger's nods to the people linking to his or her stuff), and blogrolls (an array of links to other, likeminded blogs and their most recent posts). Because the blogging community is so richly interlinked, it is still one of the purest expressions of what Sergey Brinn and Larry Page believed when they first developed the Google search-engine algorithm: That the links among websites are "votes" for the quality and nature of the content on the web. Those votes help determine what emerges atop the search-engine results.

Yes, virtually all sites are interconnected with others on the web, but the blogosphere is especially democratic with its links, less motivated by profit than are ecommerce sites. Blogs are topic-specific, creating—in the eyes of a search-engine spider—overlapping niches of hubs of authority, spokes of interconnections. The structure plays perfectly into the algorithm of Google and the other major search engines.

Like any media frenzy, the fawning over blogs was overdone. A huge number of blogs created every day quickly become ghost towns: rarely posted to, virtually unvisited, uncommented upon, and untagged. Like tumbleweeds rolling across its neglected pages, the only signs of life are those now ubiquitous Google Adwords or other paid ads.

Gartner analyst Adam Sarner gauges the number of "dead, abandoned blogs" at a mind-numbing *200 million*.[1] *Technorati* tells us some 120,000 new blogs are being born every single day[2]—but that's a decline from the peak, and there's evidence that some 25% of brand-new blogs arrive DOA and are never revisited by their creators.

Based on that level of churn, Gartner predicts the blog phenomenon will soon top off at around 100 million active blogs and decline due to the novelty wearing off. Blog creation will also give way in some measure to new, easy-to-use, and potentially more interactive forms like social network and wiki platforms, which we'll discuss later.

But neglected sites are simply a natural side effect of the tidal wave of creativity and productivity. The power of blog software is that publishing web content became simple and free, for everyone. The explosion of content was enormous and, like most trends on the internet, exponential. We should no more be discouraged by abandoned sites than we would be by crumpled sketches, dusty plans, and prototypes in some vast and humming artists' collective.

There is today a vast supply of high quality blogs on nearly any subject you can name. The format is perfectly suited for timely and unvarnished posts, brief and straight to the point. Blogs can provide previously impossible access to niche authors, scholars, pundits, speakers, and authorities we've come to respect. They can be free-flowing conversations, inspired by (and linking to) other content on the web, and commented upon by their readers. Because blogs are designed for daily posting, when they find their audience, readers tend to be faithful, visiting favorite blogs on *Technorati*, or subscribing to RSS feeds daily.

A Few Web 2.0 Definitions

RSS: for "Really Simple Syndication"—this technology delivers blog posts and any other content in a highly portable form, so they may be read in a user's personalized homepage or "feed reader" software.

WIDGETS: Small, freestanding programs—pieces of HTML and programming code—that can be pasted into any web page. They use JavaScript, DHTML, Flash, or other language to carry out some dynamic action. Web visitor counters, mini games, clocks, calendars, horoscopes, weather forecasts, and stock tickers are all examples of common widget applications. They may also be called "web widgets," "snippets" or "modules," and Google likes to call them "gadgets."

SaaS: "Software as a Service"—Software applications that are hosted on the internet and delivered on demand, through a web browser. SaaS is the Web 2.0 answer to the traditional software model of shrink-wrapped products, installed on a user's PC or on the local network.

When they first emerged, blogs were of a limited, standardized format: daily posts on a single page, sequential links to archived postings, and visitor comments. Today, the variety of blog-authoring tools has expanded, and the addition of new widgets and design themes has given bloggers great control over the look and feel of their sites. In addition, a whole slew of new just-add-water web platforms have sprung up, so the hopeful web publisher is no longer limited to a daily journal format.

▓ Online Communities, Social Media, and Networking

On social media websites like MySpace, Facebook, Orkut, Classmates, and others, individual users create and personalize their profiles, establish "friend" connections with other users, create, and respond to content. The host sites grow exponentially due to the network effect.

Facebook, for instance, is growing stratospherically. It hit the 50-million user mark in November 2007, and is adding about 6 million a month. That's a couple of dozen new users in the time it took me to type this paragraph. I'm a slow typist, yes, but you get the picture.

MySpace remains the biggest social network, with over 110 million users.

While word-of-mouth and invitations have fueled the member growth of these platforms, open technology is also poised to make them more dynamic and faster growing. Since Facebook opened its platform to third-party developers, over 2,000 Facebook applications have been launched.

Business networking site LinkedIn is opening itself to outside developers, with a focus on integrating with business SaaS applications like Salesforce, and facilitating development of widgets of interest to its audience, like hooking into business events and conferences.

These online social networks have become, for many, the new public square. Both individuals and companies need to participate, not just to be part of the conversation, but also to control their personal and company brand identity. The idea: create profiles for yourself, and your brand, before an unconnected party does. For musicians, authors, speakers, pop-culture figures, or anyone whose "brand" is their personal reputation, the social media sites are vitally important. Your profiles should link to your website. Increasingly, personal profiles from MySpace, Facebook, LinkedIn, Zoominfo, and even Amazon are appearing highly in search results for searches on people's names and even business names.

If you get the Zeitgeist of the site, active and responsible participation helps you connect with your customers and prospects. If your brand and its offerings make a strong connection to the lifestyle and values of your customers, they will increasingly want to find you online, in the places they hang out, and "friend" you. If you're in B2B, LinkedIn can help you generate business leads.

But will you sell a lot of products from any of these social media sites? No. For that goal, your time will be better rewarded doing search-engine optimization or tuning up your search-engine advertising. Still, your social media presence is increasingly important. More personal connections to more customers is a good thing. And the ones you friend in the social media are likely your best evangelists—people who are by nature among the more active, well-connected, and opinion-making people online.

SuperViva.com is a community for people to develop and share "life lists," resolutions, and things-to-do-lists, and compare notes and draw inspiration from others in the community. Nike Plus is a community where runners can log their runs, download tunes for their iPods, and interact with each other.

Companies large and small are putting social tools to work on their websites. *Internet Retailer* profiled a social network called BodySpace, launched by Bodybuilding.com, which lets users post photos and videos of themselves, save and monitor their workout goals, and blog about their progress.[3]

"There is no doubt our community and social networking offerings are making a big difference for sales and conversion," said Ryan DeLuca, Bodybuilding.com's CEO. "Since we added BodySpace, our average order size is up nearly $10 to $92.41, and our conversion rate is 8%, up from 7% a year ago. That one percentage point is huge."

While Facebook gained tons of attention and Web 2.0 "street cred" by opening up its system to outside developers, Google OpenSocial aims to do something similar but on its own terms. Google's own Orkut social network hasn't really taken off in North America. But OpenSocial hopes to change the playing field by leveraging not just Orkut, but by enabling a network of networks; OpenSocial lets developers build new social network applications by hooking into the friends lists and update feeds of Orkut and a slew of other community platforms, including Friendster, hi5, LinkedIn, MySpace, Ning, Oracle, and Salesforce.com.

If your product or service lends itself to video, you should be posting to YouTube. Most of what is watched online is noncommercial—hilarious, lewd, newsy, scandalous, or ridiculous stuff. When it comes to commercial content, all the hype goes to funny, viral videos like Smirnoff Raw Tea's preppy rap, and replaying of popular TV ads. But if you practice direct marketing, think about the niche markets interested in what you do. A well-done, straightforward instructional video on how to bake challah bread, or an infomercial on a new power tool, will likely find relevant viewers, and do more for your sales of cookbooks or plunge-cut saws than a funny but irrelevant clip. Again, the power of this sort of media comes when individual users rate, comment upon, link to, and forward links about your video to like-minded people in their online social networks.

Outside of the mainstream, general interest networks are myriad others focusing on areas like business networking, dating, photo- and video-sharing and more. Consider the case of AdultFriendFinder, and its network of dating sites. The privately held company bills itself as "The World's Largest Sex & Swinger Personals Community," with over 130 million members across thirty sites. A *Business 2.0* article[4] pointed out the company has revenues of well over $200 million a year.

Social networks have been the focus of much media hype, takeover money, and word-of-mouth curiosity. But the "next big thing" is a fast-moving target, and former social media darlings like Friendster have plunged off the radar. Recently, MySpace membership has contracted, and engagement—the measure of usage minutes per active member—is on the wane. While many have been beating the drum about the promise of social media advertising, the industry's first forays into "monetizing" its members have been awkward, to say the least, marked by inherent tensions between commerce and the privacy expectations of users.

None of that is to suggest that social networks are a flash in the pan—they are here to stay, and more and more of our social and business lives will play out in cyberspace rather than physical space. But like anything else, social media sites will have to negotiate a landscape of shrinking attention spans, wariness of advertising, and protectiveness of privacy.

▓ Virtual Worlds

Sometimes lumped into the broader "social network" category, online multiplayer games deserve their own classification. Second Life, World of Warcraft, and other online games combine 3-D animation, and social interaction and game play into a totally new phenomenon.

They go by the unwieldy acronyms MMOGs ("massively multiplayer online games") or MMORPGs ("massively multiplayer online role-playing games"). Between them, they have tens of millions of players.

Adults are not the only denizens of virtual worlds; with Club Penguin, Neopets, Webkinz, and smaller sites like Barbie Girls, there are tens of millions of kids playing these games online. Viacom recently committed $100 million to developing its Neopets and other Nickelodeon online kids gaming properties.

"Particularly in the kids' space, with more than 86% of kids 8 to 14 gaming online, we see great momentum for online casual gaming," said Cyma Zarghami, President, Nickelodeon Kids and Family Group.

Many marketers are asking themselves whether they should participate in these Virtual Worlds—and if so, how. There are basically two ways to be involved: (1) invest time in playing the game and being part of the community, and (2) advertise or create branded in-world experiences.

It's safe to say that nobody should be doing the latter until they have done the former. Without key members of your company really understanding the online world and its social norms and styles, it's impossible to know whether the game culture fits what your company has to offer. And it's impossible to make the pitch-perfect, sincere effort to reach out to game residents if you aren't already a comfortable participant in the virtual world.

▓ Tagging, Ranking, and Bookmarking

Digg, Reddit, StumbleUpon, del.icio.us, and other tagging sites take a democratic approach to determining what's hot and worthwhile on the web. Like something? Tag it. Hate something? Bury it or give it thumbs down. Whether it's a news item, a new product, an amateur video, a recipe, or anything else, the act of tagging something (or "Digging" or "Stumbling" it on those sites) makes it more prominent to other users. Especially to those within your online network—your friends, fans, or simply other users whose history demonstrates an affinity to your own interests and tastes.

Burying something has the opposite impact: It lowers the popularity of items you find objectionable, spammy, or just plain uninteresting. If enough users feel the same way as you do, the item will effectively disappear from the community.

Want to categorize or describe the item to yourself and others, so that you can find it (and other items like it) again? Tag it with plain English keywords.

Called "social classification" or "folksonomy," this people-powered, bottom-up organization of the web works well—and it's a radical departure from the approach that takes human editorial judgment out of the picture. Tagging sites are a Web 2.0 reinvention of the old Yahoo! Directory approach to organizing and ranking stuff on the web. Because it's built on a social model, users respond to each other's recommendations, creating friendship networks and granting authority to the most active and successful taggers.

These sites can send catchy, quirky news or other content pages soaring in popularity at nosebleed speed. They can fall just as abruptly. But you don't need to land on the homepage of Digg to make a relevant impact in your niche audience. As a publisher, if you have content that is great, unique, and interesting, put Digg and other tagging icons on the page!

▓ Wikis

Wiki, meaning "quick" in Hawaiian, is an approach to online collaboration made most famous by Wikipedia, the user-created and edited web encyclopedia.

The power of wiki-style collaboration, or "crowdsourcing," is not just that many hands make light work. A successful wiki harnesses collective intelligence: the notion that as a community, the sum is greater than its parts. Anyone can create a page, and anyone can edit anyone else's page.

Wiki software can include some duplication-checking, version-tracking, and other features to catch potential quality problems. But ultimately, the strength of wiki projects derives less from its software than from the collaborative work, review, and correction of its community members.

"Communities can build amazing things, but you have to be part of that community and you can't abuse them," said Wikipedia founder Jimmy Wales at a conference keynote.[5] "You have to be very respectful of what their needs are."

One early wiki is the Open Directory Project, or DMOZ.org, a human-edited web directory. But while ODP was a big success in the late 1990s, its editor community just couldn't keep up with the growth of new websites. Lately, ODP looks like an example of how wikis that grow on their own user-created energy can also stagnate or collapse under their own weight.

Wiki approaches have been famously and effectively applied to open-source software development, business collaboration, grassroots political campaigns, and large data collection and publishing projects like WikiHow and WikiQuotes.

We all have the ability to invite our community to help us create and edit content. You needn't build a wiki software system from scratch—some good, low-cost platforms exist, like Wikia, Zimbio, and Wetpaint, which you can use to publish collaborative websites, online magazines (wikizines) and more. You are now part of the wikisphere!

One of today's most closely watched wiki projects is Wikia Search, a collaboratively built search-engine project founded by the daddy of Wikipedia, Jimmy Wales. It joins Mahalo, another "human edited" search engine founded on wiki principles. Wikia Search's alpha launch (its first incarnation, before even beta-testing) revealed what Wales acknowledged to be poor search results—but inevitably with wikis, they must go public when only half-baked, and as Wales pointed out, they improve only through more user participation.

For anyone wanting to know more about wikis, *Wikinomics* by Don Tapscott and Anthony D. Williams is a must-read.

▦ Just Add Water

As we mentioned, blogs were the start of the instant-website phenomenon, but today they are the tip of the iceberg. Blogs are very basic daily publishing platforms, great at letting people post text and image content for the comments of others, but without much other interactivity or flexibility.

Now we have simple and in many cases free web interfaces for creating a whole range of specialized sites. It's getting easier and easier to make ever more complex and functional sites—granting even more power to the people.

GooglePages is a simple publishing and hosting tool for user-built web pages. Squidoo is a supereasy way to build a single page on any topic; eBay and Amazon stores have always been very user-friendly platforms for the average nontechnical user wanting to sell items online. Yahoo! Merchant Solutions (formerly known as Yahoo Store) is a step above in complexity, but still a very accessible option.

PopShops is an innovative affiliate-selling platform for bloggers and website owners who want to hook into the affiliate programs of some 1,000 or so merchants. The site owner embeds JavaScript or blog widgets into her site and *voila!* She has an online store of up to a 100 products.

The wiki platforms mentioned above enable anyone to kick off an online collaborative. Another really exciting development is the handful of great build-your-own social network software platforms. These free or inexpensive tools, from Ning, KickApps, and Drupal, let anyone launch a niche social site.

Ning is the brainchild of Web 1.0 wunderkind, Mosaic cocreator and Netscape founder Marc Andreesen. With it, you can create and customize your own social network website, complete with forums, photo, and video sharing, a blog, event calendars, all sorts of widgets, and support for member profiles and friend networks—all in a matter of a few hours.

▒ User-Submitted Ratings and Reviews

Today's consumers are deluged by commercial messages and jaded by their claims. But now, under the ethos of the "participatory web," consumers bypass the marketing department, cut through the hype, and talk to each other directly through user-submitted product reviews.

The industry standard is Amazon's five-star rating system and qualitative reviews, written by ordinary members whose profiles are visible to their fellow online shoppers. "Expert" reviewers still maintain some currency, as long as they appear sufficiently impartial. But it is user ratings that customers really trust. A number of studies have found word-of-mouth endorsement—the recommendations and reviews of "customers like me"—are the single biggest influence on purchasing.

Customer ratings and reviews functionality is now built into many software packages. Plus, it can be quickly and inexpensively integrated with most websites, thanks to some third-party platforms, which we'll discuss in Chapter 6.

Meanwhile, the key take-away is this: Web 2.0 websites empower their users to talk to each other, in straightforward and practical language. In the process, they create trusted content, and connect relevant products to the right customers in a way that no top-down marketing initiative ever could.

Marketers and customer-service managers alike have a lot to gain when customers talk to each other, Web 2.0 style. When a user-submitted reviewer says things like "the ending was too scary for my five year-old" or "this is a good, cheap, socket, set, but not rugged enough for industrial use," chances are you will disappoint fewer customers—and still reach the intended market as well or even better than before.

Emergence of New Authority Figures

While ratings and reviews put more authority into the hands of your customers, they also anoint new authority figures outside your control. You say your new mousetrap is the best and most innovative on earth, and your customer service unmatched. But your voice on the matter is one of many—a huge din of competing ads and content, some unapologetically subjective, some claiming objectivity, some from ad-driven middlemen or affiliates motivated by a share in the profit, some hoping to divert business from a competitor. Who's to believe?

From eBay and Amazon to LinkedIn and Digg, the web is full of features and widgets designed to help customers make sense of it all. Authority is conferred on individuals online by the volume of ratings they have made and their helpfulness to other users. From the start, eBay buyers and sellers live or die on their feedback ratings. Through Amazon's third-party merchant system, customer feedback is key to how conspicuously those merchants' products appear on Amazon results pages. On LinkedIn, Yahoo! Answers, and other platforms, user answers to questions may be rated by their helpfulness. Expertise signaled by "Best Answer" and other icons are the medals of many an online general.

Blog posts, wiki contributions, and other user-submitted content are also often subject to quality rating by other members in the community. Widgets allow MySpace and Facebook members to rate things—and each other—and determine compatibility. Hot or Not is dating (and rating) at its most basic level.

Ratings from places like Epinions and BizRate may impact what prospective customers think of your products, service, or brand. Even when bargain-hunting customers are ready to take out their credit card and buy from you, they will likely turn to their favorite shopping authorities—coupon and discount sites, or affinity sites like MyPoints or uPromise—to buy from you only after they have scooped up a discount code or collected their bonus.

Authority figures don't just factor before the purchase decision. Google Checkout and PayPal are locked in a clash of the titans to be the authority figure online shoppers turn to on their way *out* the checkout line. Knowing that a majority of customers are leery of trusting their credit card to online merchants—and that everybody is overwhelmed by remembering a teeming slew of registered-user accounts—these alternative checkout paths aim to be your trusted, one-stop online wallet. We'll get into more detail about this later, but the crux is this: It's yet another player vying for authority and influence on your customer.

And in the social media world, we wear our authority on our sleeves. Whether you're socializing or goofing around on MySpace or Facebook, or business networking on LinkedIn, your online experience and your influence is governed by who and how many your friends are.

Mashups

Online, people love to take your stuff and reformat it, maybe combine it with other data to look at it in a novel way. Google, Amazon, Alexa, Facebook, and hundreds of others have embraced this impulse by creating web services—tool kits that let outside developers reach into their data and re-present it in innovative ways. Also known as APIs (for "Application Programming Interfaces"), these are basically instructions telling outside programmers how to call on their data.

Mashups run the gamut from the helpful to the inane:

- FedSpending.org mashed with Google Charts produces a U.S. map shaded to show where Federal contracts have been awarded.
- Twitter Atlas: Microsoft Virtual Earth plus Twitter graphically overlays people's activities with their location on a world map.
- SmartRatings: A shopping tool aggregates product reviews from all over the web, and mashes them with prices.

By far the most popular web mashups are mapping applications—driven mostly by the powerful Google Maps platform. Here are the top mashup categories, according to ProgrammableWeb, the authority on mashups and APIs:

42% Mapping
10% Photos
9% Search
8% Shopping
6% Travel
5% Video
4% Sports
4% Real Estate
3% Messaging

Web developers have had a field day making creative use of APIs to present others' data on their own sites in new ways. Perhaps there is a mashup relevant to your online audience, waiting to be born on your site. Conversely, syndicating your own data out to the world gives others the opportunity to view it or republish it in their own way.

While the most sophisticated data-mashups require a developer's talents, a number of easy, browser-based mashup tools have sprung up. These enable Average Joes to get into the game of creating their own fresh web applications by combining two or more streams of data. Yahoo! Pipes, Microsoft Popfly, JackBuilder, Dapper, and Netvibes are just a few of the new environments that let nonprogrammers combine web data feeds, web pages, and functionality like Ajax or Silverlight to create brand new widgets, maps, alerts, RSS feeds, and more.

John Musser, the Seattle-based software developer and technology exec who founded ProgrammableWeb, catalogs several hundred APIs and a few thousand mashups on the site. He also blogs on the latest tools, news, and other developments in the field, "because," he says, "the world is your programmable oyster."

Link Juice

I love this term. Supposedly coined by search marketing consultant Greg Boser, "link juice" is the ranking benefit you get when someone else's site links to you.

With Google at the forefront, all the major search engines now make interlinking a core measure of a site's quality. The more links you have, and the higher the quality of sites linking to you, the more authority—and organic search rank—you will enjoy.

You'll often hear the little guy complain that his small online business has no chance with the search engines, that Google, Wikipedia, and big business are in collusion against him, and that with a capricious tweak of its algorithm, Google can shut off his lifeblood.

Organic search traffic is vital to many online businesses. Smaller ventures, which lack traditional advertising budgets, depend disproportionately on search; even the mature direct-marketing companies I've worked for often receive 60% or more of their web traffic from the search engines: about half of it related to their brand name, and the other half incremental keyword searches—the kind we aim for when we do search-engine optimization.

But if anything, the web is *more* democratic than the offline world, not less. Smaller companies often outrank huge ones, for a number of reasons:

1. Big companies shy away from the keyword-rich (to some, spammy) text copy that is still a big part of search-engine optimization.

2. Big companies' graphic designers prefer handsome images to HTML text, anyhow.
3. Big companies often use sophisticated ecommerce platforms whose dynamic URLs can still pose a problem to search-engine spiders.
4. Because of the importance placed on links, the best-ranking site isn't necessarily the biggest—it's the one that is most deeply involved in the fabric of the web, the quirkiest, or most newsworthy, the most passionately discussed and linked to. That could be you. Why not?

▦ Going Viral

The network effect of the web guarantees that when something starts happening online, it gets bigger in a hurry—whether it's a career-ending celebrity video, a free email platform, an urban legend, or a virus. Some great books have been written on the subject of products, brands, and fads going viral, online and in the world at large. The best are *Unleashing the Ideavirus* (Seth Godin), *The Tipping Point* (Malcolm Gladwell), and *Made to Stick* (Chip and Dan Heath).

What is the problem here? Your boss is going to read one of these books, march into your office, and tell you to come up with a viral marketing campaign. "Viral" in this context means exponentially fast-moving, where each person touched by the campaign spreads the word to more than one other person. In preinternet days, most marketing investments produced linear growth. But with the frictionless ease of email and hyperlinking, consumers on the web spread word-of-mouth at an exponential rate. However, you can't just set out to create something viral. Instead, set out to create something terrific, new and worth talking about. If it is all those things, maybe the world and the web will take it viral for you.

People don't spam their friends. If they're going to buzz about and link to and pass along material, it will likely be something that appeals either to their sense of humor, their libido, their politics, or causes. If your stuff is more mundane, it's a tough order—but it can be done if you're approach is sincere.

Seth Godin points to the viral success of Blendtec on YouTube: hilarious but authentic low-budget "Will it Blend?" videos, featuring Tom Dickson, the lab-coated president of the company, successfully blending everything from marbles to hockey pucks.

"Remarkable almost never costs a lot," says Godin. "Blendtec has spent less than $1,000 to reach more than 20 million people with their videos. But there's no way they would work if the blender was lousy. Too many people jump ahead to the sexy part, without realizing that you don't get there without a product that's worth talking about."[6]

You can help the process, too, by removing the friction—the impediments that enthusiasts might face in spreading the word. Put your remarkable stuff into video form, and create RSS feeds or APIs, so your data gets out there. Display social tagging icons from Digg, Redditt, and others, and forward-to-a-friend links on your pages.

Another aspect of viral marketing is that it's possible (and probably preferable) for an idea to go viral within a relevant niche community without penetrating the mass culture. People may eagerly pass a sugarfree cookie recipe to the diabetics they know, a doggie fashion show video to their dog-loving friends, or a "Top 10 Online Marketing Blunders" list to all their marketing colleagues. Sure, it's a humble campaign unlikely to be talked about in the *Wall Street Journal*, but as Godin points out, it's better to reach a hundred of the right people than a million of the wrong people.

Microsites are good places for content or applications you hope might go viral. Burger King's 2004 "Subservient Chicken" interactive video microsite was an early, goofy, and virally popular riff on the company's "Have it Your Way" slogan. Beer.com's virtual bartenders are of the same concept.

CareerBuilder's talking Monk-e-Mail has generated over 110 million messages, which are passed along at a rate of 20% to 25%. For Career-Builder, it's principally about brand building, and echoing their "Working with Monkeys" TV ad campaign. Because the campaign and the email platform are one and the same, the Monk-e-Mail phenomenon eliminates a lot of "friction," that is, obstacles for people to tell others. As a result, it spreads incredibly fast.

OfficeMax's interactive ElfYourself microsite received 40 million visits in the 2006 holiday season and helped lift traffic to the OfficeMax website some 20%.

Smirnoff's Raw Tea "Tea Partay" parody rap video has been viewed almost 4 million times on YouTube, and helped propel the beverage to lead its category in sales.

Viral success stories like these don't rely on big, mass-market advertising budgets to reach millions of eyeballs. They start small, and depend on inherent appeal to generate enough word-of-mouth "buzz" that each new round of fans is exponentially bigger than the previous.

Being Flamed, Spoofed, and Cybersquatted

Okay, getting flamed is a quaint term from the Jurassic era of online chatrooms, but it's more relevant to companies now than it ever was. As mentioned, customers pay ever more heed to the opinions, reviews, and ratings of ordinary people like them. When disaffected customers take a mind to trash you at various online venues, it's remarkable how prolific they can be.

Keep in mind the increasing reliance of users on search engines. Even when people know your URL and intend to go straight to you, a goodly number of them type your name into a search engine instead of bothering with all those w's and dotcoms. Many others just set their address bar to resolve keywords in a search engine.

A Nielsen/NetRatings study[7] found that the top search terms, by volume, are dominated by searches for sites by name. "There are two types of online searchers that type a Web site's URL into a search engine rather than into the browser's address bar: Those inexperienced enough not to appreciate the difference between the two, and those that are so experienced they have become habituated to using the search engine as their portal to the internet," said Ken Cassar, Nielsen/NetRatings chief analyst. "Whether this behavior is driven by ignorance or savvy, the end result is the same: The search engine is the focal point of the online experience for internet users across the spectrum."

When one of the top search-engine results for searches on your brand name is a slam from an alienated customer, your brand image is taking a body blow every time a hopeful customer comes looking for you. For example, currently one of the top-ranked Google results for a "Comcast" search is an embarrassing YouTube video of a hapless Comcast technician, on-hold with his company's own tech support, and fast asleep on the couch of a customer who filmed the whole thing and posted it. Not good.

With the advent of social media, it's even easier to step into a minefield. First, there's the sin of omission: failing to establish accounts on the major and even minor social networks, and thereby allowing squatters and pranksters to create high-profile accounts slamming your brand or making it look bad. That's not to say that your participation in online social networks should be aimed at taking individual consumers out of the equation! For one thing, it "ain't gonna happen." For another, one of the most powerful business forces of Web 2.0 social networking is to unleash consumers' honest and passionate tributes to, and reviews of, your products and services.

But you don't want to be in the position of, say, Anheuser Busch, and find that the MySpace username *Budweiser*—with some 16,000 friends— is a dubious and somewhat official-looking tribute page reading, in part: "Being a beer built on taste, quilty [sic] and most of all tradition, Budweiser encorporates [sic] all aspects of beer drinking needed to keep its drinkers happy, satisfifed [sic], and DRUNK."

Critical voices about your business are also part of the online conversation. And should bad press and word-of-mouth ever reach crisis proportions, the golden rules for crisis response are truer than ever in Web 2.0—and they need to be deployed at the speed of light. Companies must understand both the positive and negative sides of viral growth on the internet. When a potential crisis emerges, today's companies need to be completely upfront, and immediately start to remedy a problem, be it a product recall, severing a controversial relationship, or what have you.

Jennifer Laycock, a mom and breastfeeding advocate, who edits Search Engine Guide by day and the Lactivist blog by night, supports her breast-feeding site by selling funny tee shirts like "That's my baby's lunch you're staring at."

One day, Jennifer received a stern cease-and-desist letter from lawyers for the National Pork Board, regarding a shirt emblazoned with the slogan "The Other White Milk." They were unamused by the shirt's similarity with their "The Other White Meat" trademark, and insisted she stop selling the shirt, destroy all unsold inventory of it, and take other measures. Rather than roll over, Jennifer fought back, sharing the nasty letter—and her own indignant and hilarious take on the whole issue—with her blog readers. Almost immediately, the blogosphere turned up the heat: Jennifer's blog post was linked to, commented upon, and posted about by hundreds of readers and other bloggers. It was Dugg hundreds of times, and tagged on del.icio.us and Reddit. Angry supporters rallied to her side, emailing and calling the Pork Board (whose executives' names and contact info Jennifer helpfully posted on her blog). The controversy made its way onto more mainstream venues like Salon.com and Brandweek.com.

Law firms volunteered to defend Jennifer against the Pork Board, *pro bono*. Chief among them was the Electronic Freedom Foundation, which bills itself as "the leading civil liberties group defending your rights in the digital world." Jennifer's hosting company threw free bandwidth at the huge traffic increases to her site.

As with many miniviral campaigns on the web, this one was a perfect storm: partly a moral crusade, and partly just plain laughable. "National Pork Board Stumbles into Hornet's Nest of Bloggers," posted *Information-Week*, while *Search Engine Roundtable* put it more wryly: "Search Engine Industry Blogger, Jennifer Laycock, Ordered to Remove Her Shirt." It helped that she had two natural constituencies: tech-savvy search-engine geeks from her professional world, and the parenting and lactation community of her personal life.

Suddenly it no longer looked like such a straightforward trademark infringement play from the Corporate Law 101 playbook. It was starting to look like the pork industry versus breastfeeding and motherhood.

For the record, the National Pork Board did the right thing: They quickly dropped their attorney's threats, the CEO sent an apology to Jennifer, and individual Pork Board executives and staff even dug into their pockets to support the charity of Jennifer's choice, Mother's Milk Bank of Ohio. No doubt the organization was mortified that a boilerplate letter from their law firm landed them on the wrong side of a powerful and emotional issue. Jennifer Laycock applauded them for their resolution of the affair.

It's worth noting that any organization that maintains and invests in trademarks has not just an interest in, but a legal obligation to defend those marks. But the point is, any organization doing business today needs to recalibrate its interactions with the outside world.

No longer can you assume a spurned or dissatisfied customer will simply go away. They just may well be among the small but potent fraction of web users who are energetic content creators: well connected, active bloggers, evangelists, and gadflies whose causes and opinions grow virally across the web.

Importantly, the pork industry group's black eye didn't fade when the PR crisis blew over. While bad broadcast news cycles are measured in days, and bad press coverage gets carried out with the recycling, unflattering web pages are forever. Even today, four of the top ten Google results for "National Pork Board" point to pages about the tee-shirt controversy.

▨ Confusingly Similar

It has always been prudent to register all possible variations of your domain name to foil cybersquatters. But today, by syndicating their paid search ads, with a revenue-share of pennies on the click, the major search engines provide a financial incentive for an entire ecosystem of sites to attract traffic meant for another destination. The search engines are at pains to improve the quality of these "content networks." But cybersquatters and "AdSense spammers" still proliferate. And you yourself, if you maintain an online affiliate program, need to be eternally vigilant lest unsavory affiliates register confusingly similar domains to your own, detour customers by advertising your brand name, frame your site in their own iframe, spoof your outbound email program with unsolicited emails of their own—and countless other scams, motivated by the revenue share you offer—which have the effect of making your brand look cheesy.

Alas, there is no easy prescription for controlling your brand image in cyberspace, but awareness is the first step, and good citizenship online and off is the best defense. Inevitably, some unflattering content about you is already online and more is on the way. But there are only ten spots on the first page of results, and by actively and positively engaging with the online community, you greatly better your chances that they'll all be brand-positive.

▨ (Even More) Power to the People

If the power shift I've just described sounds a little bewildering, brace yourself. It's going to increase. In its "Teens and Social Media" report, the *Pew Internet* and the *American Life Project*[8] recently found that almost two out of three online teenagers are now creating online content. Some 64% of online teenagers ages 12 to 17 engage in blogging, photo sharing, or other content creation.

> *Girls continue to dominate most elements of content creation. Some 35% of all teen girls blog, compared with 20% of online boys, and 54% of wired girls post photos online compared with 40% of online boys. Boys, however, do dominate one area—posting of video content online. Online teen boys are nearly twice as likely as online girls (19% vs. 10%) to have posted a video online . . .*

The Pew research also identifies some 28% of teens as "super-communicators—teens who have a host of technology options for dealing with family and friends, including traditional landline phones, cell phones, texting, social network sites, instant messaging, and email."

The message is simple: Gen Y has grown up spontaneously interacting with the web, freely publishing their own material and their responses to others. The Web 2.0 landscape already empowers the ordinary netizen, and that trend can be expected to gain momentum.

2 ■ ■ ■

Pull Media, Not Push

We've just looked at some of the ways ordinary people are calling the shots in Web 2.0. So far, our focus has been on users posting or rating content, creating links, reviews, and passing your content along virally. Another key aspect of Web 2.0 is that users are opting in for custom messages and content they want—and turning an increasingly deaf ear to what they do not.

■ Decline of Interruption Marketing

Seth Godin coined the term "Interruption Marketing" to describe the traditional direct marketing that regularly interrupts what you, the customer, are trying to do. They're the television ads in the middle of your favorite show, print ads in the midst of an article, junk mail in your mailbox, and telemarketing on your phone. The era of interruption marketing is out. The new wave, wrote Godin, is Permission Marketing: messages relevant to the receiver and specifically requested by them.

   Don't expect the death of interruption marketing anytime soon, but the writing may be on the wall: in 2007, virtually *all* of the growth in advertising spending came from online advertising. Traditional offline media, overall, was flat. Categories like print actually saw a decline. In the United States, the national do-not-call list has swelled to 150 million Americans making their phones off-limits to telemarketers.[1]

Spam email is the real poster child of unwanted advertising. The CAN-SPAM law took aim at unsolicited email in 2003, prompting legitimate marketers to follow best practices regarding opt-in policies (asking the customer clearly whether she wants to join or opt out of your emailing program), and handling unsubscribed requests, etc. Sometimes the FBI is able to slap the cuffs on a big spammer living within U.S. borders. But that law likely had much less effect on unwanted email than did the efforts of spam-fighting technology companies. Today, *though an estimated 95% of all email messages are spam,*[2] email filtering algorithms snag much of it at several points in the pipeline: at ISPs, on corporate networks, online email platforms and installed email clients. Nearly all the offending material is snuffed out before it even reaches our in-boxes. There is still no shortage of emails touting Botox or Nigerian bank-transfer scams, but it could be a lot worse.

However, there's evidence that a merchant's definition of spam and that of the average consumer may be worlds apart. While a merchant figures she's operating within the rules as long as she obeys CAN-SPAM, the consumer doesn't read the fine print: to the consumer, any irritating, unwanted commercial message feels like spam—even if they technically "agreed" to receive it. The feeling extends to generally desired emails that are sent too frequently. That's why, just a few years after CAN-SPAM, Congress is considering a national do-not-email list.

▦ Rise of User-Requested Marketing

The marketers among us may be feeling a little uneasy. How are we to grow revenues if people keep TiVo-ing past our commercials: we can't telemarket, print readerships are stagnant, and our mail-order catalogs are drowning in a rising sea of competing titles? The answer looks easy. Responding to a 2007 Internet Retailer survey, almost 60% of marketers said they planned to do more search-engine advertising.

Search Advertising

The profusion of "sponsored results" on every search engine is getting a little garish, but it's fair to call paid-search a form of permission marketing. After all, the user has signaled her interest in what the advertisers have to offer, by searching for it by name. And by clicking on a particular ad—based on its brand name, say, or its ad copy or position—she has doubly qualified herself as an interested customer. At least on Google and Yahoo!, the popularity of each ad is tabulated in a "quality score" that results in irrelevant ads falling lower on the page or being suppressed altogether.

In this scenario, customer and advertiser alike should both be happy with the connection. Ad spending is a clear indication that advertisers like what they see. As for searchers (although they are generally more likely to click organic results than paid ones) that preference varies greatly by search engine, user gender, etc.

In an iProspect study,[3] for instance, Google users much preferred organic listings over paid results, by a margin of 72% to 28%. MSN users were the complete opposite, with 71% favoring paid listings over organic results (29%).

Loyalty Emails and e-Newsletters

The other big winner among advertising media has been email marketing. Not spam, mind you, but the responsible, user-requested "loyalty programs" mandated by CAN-SPAM. A whopping 83% of marketers surveyed chose email marketing to their house list as the most important advertising medium they will use.[4] For most companies I'm familiar with, email is the most profitable marketing channel. It's no wonder: your opt-in email list is a precious resource, a database of your best customers who have given you permission to reconnect with them on an ongoing basis. They expect to be given relevant messages and some special treatment: member-only discounts, sneak-peeks at new products, access to exclusive sales. If you deliver on those expectations, and don't fatigue your people by overmailing to them, your email program will be healthy indeed.

Another permission-based outreach you can make to your customers is to offer informative editorial content, in the form of e-newsletters. While these need to be truly interesting, and primarily editorial, they can contain a few new- or sale-product links—and even when they do not, they have a tendency to drive commercial traffic simply by reminding your customers that you're still alive.

You are well-suited to offer a newsletter if your market niche is peopled by real enthusiasts, like gardeners or other hobbyists, or if your marketplace is subject to frequent change—picture the travel business, where travel deals and hot new destinations come and go with regularity. B2B businesses are almost always good candidates to publish regular online newsletters, and they should also develop relevant white papers, case studies or other primary research about their industry. These are usually produced as pdfs, but you owe it to yourself to also offer HTML and

RSS versions, for the sake of better interlinking and transmission to the outside world.

Although the infrastructure of today's web is doing a better job of stopping unsolicited commercial email, most of us are daily faced with email inboxes more crammed than ever. Business and personal email communication has ballooned. And since just about every online merchant worth his salt has enrolled you in his email program, you're receiving more promotional emails than ever. Some of the crush is due to increasing frequency of promotional email. While early programs gravitated to monthly frequency, marketers have found they can increase to every week or two, and more frequently during peak seasons.

The only antidote to the overcrowded in-box is for you to keep your permission-based messages as useful, relevant, and valuable to your customers as you possibly can. Industry standards vary greatly, but if you're getting 20% or better open rates, 10% click-through rates, and keeping your unsubscribe rates below 1%, you can pat yourself on the back: your customers are relatively interested in your messages, and relatively responsive to their content once they open them. If your numbers are worse, you need to go back to the drawing board and make your program deliver on the promises that made your customers opt in to begin with.

Alerts and Feed Subscriptions

If your market lends itself to the practice, you can get visitors to subscribe to brief email alerts whenever a particular event occurs: a new blog post occurs, there's a news article on a particular topic, a stock hits a target price, there's a change to a particular web page, a rare item becomes available, or someone bids on an item. Social networks have seized on the friends "news feed" or in-box alerts to connect to members on or off their platforms.

Many merchants have discovered the power of special event reminders, occasions like birthdays and anniversaries.

Alerts are still most commonly delivered as emails, but RSS and Atom syndication have really taken off (Atom is another data format that does the same thing as RSS: It makes data portable, so users can "pull" it from publishers whenever and wherever they want to view it—rather than having to always return to the source website). Amazon lets you subscribe to RSS feeds of best sellers, new releases, and Movers & Shakers in any category or subcategory you choose. Amazon also lets visitors subscribe to "available to order" notifications for upcoming books, music, and out-of-stock products.

eHobbies offers 70,000 hobby products including model trains and rockets, die-cast cars, plastic model kits, science experiments, and more. To keep passionate hobbyists aware of their ever-changing inventory, eHobbies offers a number of RSS feeds—one of new items, another for best sellers, and another of items coming back in stock.

Whether you build an alert-triggering system into your own web application, or let users subscribe to timely content whenever it's published, you take your website into Web 2.0 territory: You provide exactly what your audience wants, when it's most relevant.

Take your best, most interesting data—your new-product announcements, newly on-sale items, new discount codes, a daily news blast, how-to advice, latest user ratings and reviews, award-winning customer-supplied photos, daily blog posts, you name it—and let your customers subscribe to it.

Put your data into a feed format like RSS or Atom, display the RSS or Atom button, and your most interested customers now no longer have to revisit your site to see what's new; they can view it on their favorite feed-reader, plug it into their MyYahoo!, Google, Facebook, browser-based aggregators like NewsGator Online, and elsewhere. Often, users have no idea they're reading RSS data: The same technology is used to spread new blog posts and online press releases across countless news-oriented sites, or to display personalized stock quotes, news highlights, sports scores, and other information on custom pages.

Customers have given you a place on their homepage. That's an awesome compliment—and it puts the onus on you to deliver great content.

Ecommerce veteran Ethan Holland was an early adopter of RSS, offering a feed back in 2004 when he was ecommerce director of Burpee Seeds. The feeds reached 100,000 of the company's most interested customers at a cost of almost nothing. Today, as eCommerce Director at Jewelry Television, Ethan employs an RSS feed of "Daily Top of the Hour Specials," which is updated every 15 minutes.

Feeds delivered over instant-messaging systems, pagers, PDAs, and cell phones are a burgeoning field. The technology is a little different, usually involving SMS (Short Messaging Service), better known as text-messaging, but the effect is the same: reaching your audience with timely, desired information over the device of their choice. A number of services like GoLive! Mobile, and MessageBuzz have sprung up to help companies collect and manage opt-in lists of their mobile customers, create and send text-message campaigns and contests, offer downloadable ring-tones, and other goodies. Some will even build small WAP (Wireless Application Protocol) sites—mobile websites designed to work on a mobile phone browser, and to serve as landing pages for your SMS marketing efforts.

Feeds offer a couple of advantages over emails and alerts: they don't need to contend with overcrowded mailboxes, for one. And because the format is universal, an entire ecosystem of feed-enabled sites can and do pick up your feed. That means more exposure across the web, more chance to be "Dugg," and more chance of emerging in organic search engine results. You may show up in unexpected places; it may take some adjustment to the idea of "giving away" your content. But in Web 2.0 sharing your best information is a good thing, and it will come back to help you.

Widgets

Widgets are small applications that can be easily embedded into blogs and other websites. These are usually Flash or JavaScript programs, which can run wherever their code is pasted—it is easy to cut-and-paste to add a widget to almost any web page. Widgets run the gamut from daily trivia questions, countdowns, world clocks, calendars, to-do lists, cute animations, top ten lists, breaking news, mini analytics tools, and search utilities.

The attraction for ordinary web users is that widgets can really spice up their personal pages, be they portals, blogs, social media profiles, or whatever. For the developers who create popular widgets, the payoff might be traffic, product sales, brand recognition, or advertising revenue, depending on the widget.

Facebook's open-platform initiative, which kicked off in May 2007, encouraged an incredible surge of widget development, by third-party programmers and designers, which has ultimately been great for the user experience of those teeming millions of Facebook users. But the widget developers have benefited too: the ratings firm Quantcast reported that leading widget makers like Slide, RockYou, and HOTorNOT experienced a dramatic and lasting traffic increase after deploying each new widget.

Recently, in a single month, about 87 million people in the United States used an online widget, according to comScore Media Metrix.[5] Google offers some 14,000 widgets (or "gadgets" in Google parlance) for use on GooglePages, iGoogle, YouTube, and other customizable Google properties.

Still, *JupiterResearch* finds that awareness of widgets is still fairly low: fewer than 40% of online users were familiar with widgets.[6] Around 25% reported using them. But chances, are, many people are using widgets without even knowing it. And it's young people who have been the most aggressive adopters and sharers of cool widgets.

"Social networking sites have greatly contributed to the viral spread of widgets," said *Jupiter* media analyst Barry Parr. *Jupiter* found that online users between the ages of 18 and 24 were six times more likely to get widgets from friends than from the companies that created them.

Although widgets can be spread across many millions of page views with ease, and can move tons of visitors back to a developer's site in search of more cool free stuff, it's unclear where the financial model is going. There are signs that widgets will become advertising-driven. Google now distributes widget ads in its Content Network—so merchants can create interactive advertising within widgets, to be spread virally across the internet.

Similarly, the shopping portal Mpire has introduced WidgetBucks, a pay-per-click widget ad network. Mpire gadgets include price-checkers, bestseller lists, and other product-searching applets that would make financial sense for affiliates of merchants like Target, Wal-Mart, Best Buy, NewEgg, Macy's, and Gap.[7]

"As opposed to content-oriented widgets, we offer widgets that make money, the Holy Grail of the widget revolution," said Mpire's Dean Jutilla.

User-Customized Pages

As mentioned above, web users can now pick and choose what syndicated content they want to view on their "My" page, and where. There is now a huge variety of syndicated content, as well as useful or amusing little applications (widgets), which can be plugged into any customizable page. Suddenly, blogs aren't the only way that nontechnical folks can instantly create their own websites. Now crowds of platforms are available enabling everyone to build web pages quickly and at no cost. Google Pages and Squidoo are two such platforms: very cool, full featured, and fun, letting people create their own content and also able to hook effortlessly into widgets, photos shared on Flickr, videos on YouTube, RSS feed content, product search results on Amazon, etc. By syndicating your information, and by posting your own material at Flickr and YouTube, your online footprint may now extend further, to the personal sites of enthusiasts in your market.

After a global customer survey, the cell phone and electronics company Nokia recently predicted that by 2012, fully 25% of all entertainment will be created, edited, and shared by individuals and their social networks rather than by media companies.[8]

"People will have a genuine desire not only to create and share their own content, but also to remix it, mash it up and pass it on within their peer groups—a form of collaborative social media," said Mark Selby, Nokia's Vice President of Multimedia.

▓ Personalization

In Web 2.0, customers expect a more personalized shopping experience. When they return to a store they frequent, they expect to be remembered, their data stored for quick checkout, and products recommended based on some understanding of who they are. Increasingly, they gravitate to rich, interactive shopping tools that let them customize their purchases, select and preview product options, combine elements, or personalize them with their name, gift-wrapping, and gift card options.

Since customer segmentation is such a crucial aspect to marketing in general, and since a website is such a data-processing machine, the notion of online customer segmentation is a longstanding one. Amazon is the granddaddy of the field and probably its ablest practitioner. The idea is that your online performance benefits when your website can respond to customers' personal preferences, browsing behavior, buying histories, etc.

Ecommerce platforms capable of delivering personalized, user-targeted experience have become dramatically more affordable. Features once found only in million-dollar websites can now be found in mid-market ecommerce platforms. Most platforms now provide the basics of stored customer addresses, and welcome return visitors by name, thanks to cookies—small text files created by a website that store identifying information on a user's computer. That's no small help: Just that simple "Welcome back, Jane!" message can lift conversion rate and average order significantly.

Sophisticated algorithmic cross-selling tools, or recommendation engines like Amazon's ubiquitous "people who bought X also bought Y" can still be a complicated and pricey proposition to develop. But most ecommerce platforms allow merchandisers to manually assign cross-sells based on what they know about product affinities, or to establish logical connections between products. SLI "Learning Search" software applies the same principles to search results, using history to develop trees of related categories, rank most popular items higher, respond correctly to misspellings, or suggest similar search terms.

If your ecommerce platform doesn't have logic rules of its own, third-party software like Mercado and Endeca can integrate with your ecommerce platform to display certain content based on searches or other user behavior. Customers performed an onsite search using the word "sale" or "cheap"? Display a banner promoting the closeout category. They bailed out of your shopping cart when they saw your shipping prices? Display a free-shipping offer.

Just For You

More powerful than identifying site-wide customer preferences, is truly homing in on the individual customer. Amazon-style recommendation engines have been joined by similar approaches from Netflix, which invites customers to choose favorite genres and rate each movie they see, and then looks for correlations among movies. Netflix further correlates customers with those whose ratings reveal similar tastes. Yahoo! Radio uses its listeners' own ratings to deliver more relevant playlists.

The technology has long existed to deliver custom website experiences based on attributes like the referring page, query strings used, past purchases, recently viewed items, or profile of logged-in customers. Simple IP-address detection can enable a website to know your geographical location—displaying, for instance, mortgage rates or medical insurance policies available in your home state. This practice is seen more frequently in targeting of ads on ad-sponsored sites.

Few people argue about the benefits of basic personalization: welcoming visitors by name; greeting them by name in in-house email campaigns; displaying previously viewed or wish-listed items. Beyond the basics, though, there's little consensus on what customizations are best to deliver customers what they want—without inadvertently hiding from them discoveries they might be eager to make. Usability guru Jakob Nielsen, for instance, has long argued that fancy personalization algorithms are no substitute for well-designed navigation and effective on-site search.

Perhaps the most powerful personalization tools are not algorithms applied by the merchant, but greater use of the user-driven customizations we just discussed—letting visitors select widgets and RSS feeds for their own custom page.

The "made for me" market of user-customized products now runs the gamut from custom-fit clothing from Target to a T and Lands End Custom, to self-publishing site Lulu, and promotional products and tee-shirt sites galore, like CafePress and others, who let you imprint your own art or message on everything: from a wall clock to a thong.

Another attractive angle, if you offer monogrammed or other personalized products, is to use rich image technology to better preview product images with the exact style color, and personalized message the customer desires. Lenox, the manufacturer of china, crystal, gifts, and collectibles, specializes in personalized and engraved items. Lenox used Scene7 rich-media software to display dynamic images of the actual monogramming, custom birthstones, engraving or other personalization input by the customer, in the exact font, style, and color, all realistically contoured across the product.

"The response to personalization was so overwhelming that it far exceeded our expectations," said Lori Leone, Merchandising Manager. Conversion rates for personalized products increased twofold with the introduction of these dynamic preview images.[9]

During the holiday season, Lenox applied similar personalized graphics for its in-house email program. In emails featuring a personalized Christmas ornament, Lenox dynamically inscribed each recipient's first name onto the ornament image, by tying the image call to customer information pulled from the email database. Results of this visual personalization were compelling: In an A/B split test, Lenox reported a 32% lift in response rates, and a 41% increase in sales.

▓ Niches and Microsites

Rather than try to segment audiences within a larger site, many merchants are launching niche websites and microsites to serve a single customer group. BirkenstockCentral.com, which has been a leading seller of Birkenstocks for over 20 years, didn't want to dilute its brand when it branched into clogs, sandals, and shoes from other manufacturers like Keen and Chaco—so it launched GroundedSoles.com. Then, to supply comfortable shoes to people who are on their feet a lot, they launched ChefShoes.com and MedicalShoes.com. Finally came a site dedicated to leather-free footwear, VeganShoes.com. The attraction of segmenting out your product line into silos has a lot to do with the long tail of the web: When search-engines and comparative shopping exposes the same products from myriad different suppliers, and many of those suppliers are unfamiliar names to the average searcher, then the merchant must do what he can to establish his authority in his market.

Backcountry.com, specializing in camping and outdoor sports gear, has employed this niche strategy successfully by serving its snowboarding audience with a separate brand, DogFunk.com. They also launched a deep-discount site, modeled on Woot (woot.com), called Steep and Cheap.

Microsites are the extreme manifestation of niche, special-purpose websites. Created to serve a particular product, campaign, or other tightly focused goal, they're the natural outgrowth of targeted search-marketing—and, because they're memorable, they actually fit in nicely to broadcast and other campaigns.

Big media companies and consumer product manufacturers often use microsites to spotlight individual efforts that would get lost on the parent company site. The Phillips Norelco "Shave Everywhere" microsite, for instance, is dedicated to the razor that lets men do just that. McDonalds

"McMornings" microsite supports a breakfast ad campaign. Every new movie or basketball sneaker gets its own microsite.

But what flies under the radar are the microsites that can serve direct-marketers to convert search visitors to paid customers by showing exactly what they're looking for. If someone searches for women's watches, would you be better off driving them to the watches category of your online clothing, watches, jewelry, and accessory store—or would you fare better with a simplified microsite offering nothing but women's watches?

When Ion Interactive conducted a small survey of online marketers, asking, "Where do you send respondents who click on your ads?" here's what it found (results add up to greater than 100% because some marketers use more than one tactic):

- Landing pages: 75%
- Home page: 49%
- Microsites: 25%
- Deep links: 27%
- Conversion paths: 21%.

Landing pages are specially designed entry pages within an existing site. Deep links are simply existing category or product pages. Conversion paths, or conversion funnels, are a series of specially designed conversion pages distinct from the main check out or conversion path of the site as a whole. The variety of approaches currently being used is really instructional, because it reflects the fact that Web 2.0 merchants are still experimenting with how best to serve the kinds of purposeful (but impatient) shoppers in today's search-driven culture.

Ion is a big proponent of "transactional landing pages" and multistep landing experiences—clear and single-minded pages aimed squarely at getting a visitor to make an action, such as filling out an inquiry form, buying a product, joining a free trial, or downloading a white paper. Ion reports that compared to industry average conversion rates of 2.2%, its clients averaged 11%—a whopping five times the norm.

By slicing your efforts into manageable niches, you can dominate. By funneling directed searchers straight to what they're looking for and eliminating distractions, you hasten the path to purchase. This is traditional marketing advice, but the fragmented Web 2.0 landscape makes it more useful than ever.

3 ▪ ▪ ▪

The Web As Platform: The Network Is the Computer

Back when the debate was between mainframes and networked minicomputers, Sun Microsystems rallied under the slogan, "The Network is the Computer." By 2000, Tim O'Reilly and John Battelle were applying that slogan to the biggest network of all: the World Wide Web. They realized that the internetworking of millions of PCs, in an environment of soaring bandwidth, plunging storage costs, and more nimble programming languages, was the embodiment of distributed computing power.

Whether it's Google's massive server farms busily indexing and retrieving the world's information, or 3 million geeks harnessing their computers to the Search for Extraterrestrial Intelligence, the web is capable of unprecedented data processing.

On a smaller scale, applications delivered on-demand across the internet have transformed our image of software. And web-enabled cell phones and other devices have transformed our image of the web.

To top it all, open platforms and data formats now make information portable. It isn't frozen at a particular address, in a single presentation, but can be syndicated across the entire web, onto blogs, stores, and news feeds, mixed and mashed up with other data streams, repurposed for various devices. The data has been set free.

Up to this point we've talked about the trends—many of them more cultural than technical—that have put more web content creation into the hands of individuals, and allowed them to get a more personalized, on-demand version of the web. In some respects these cultural effects are almost indistinguishable from the technologies that made them possible. Flexible, interactive programming models yield a more flexible, interactive online experience.

What technological changes made Web 2.0 possible? Looking at the web as a massive computing platform, I see four attributes that make today's web distinct from the earlier era:

- Dynamic, interactive websites.
- Software in the cloud.
- High-bandwidth, rich media experiences.
- Distribution across mobile and other devices.

▨ The Power of Interactivity

Far from the brochureware of Web 1.0 days, today's websites generally serve up dynamic content. When a visitor hits a particular address, a site calls into databases of information to deliver a page custom to the particular user, the desired content, and a particular moment in time.

Dynamic sites pull information from their own local database, and can factor in the identity, history, navigation patterns, and other behavior of each visitor from stored cookies, tracking links, and log-ins. They can alter their display based on behind-the-scenes queries on the browser, device, connection speed, geographical location, and other characteristics of the visitor. A dynamic site can treat visitors differently, based on where they came from, or what they were searching for on the major search-engines that brought them in the door. Increasingly, sites also interact with third-party services—from mapping services to bestseller lists, tagging sites to social media networks—to further customize the experience to a particular user, subject matter, and time frame.

Throw in the toolbars, custom browser plug-ins, and widgets that a user can add to her personal pages and portals. Perhaps the experience is also customized, based on relationships a site-owner has struck with advertising networks and ISPs the user interacts with elsewhere on the web. The bottom line is that a Web 2.0 site is a complex, data-driven application on which no two user experiences are identical.

Interactivity isn't just about websites responding to visitors. Web-hosted data and applications are talking to each other too.

Lightweight Programming Models

I'm borrowing the phrase "lightweight programming models" from Battelle and O'Reilly's definition of Web 2.0, because it nicely sums up a number of technologies that have made for richer connections among websites and data sources, and for zippier, more interactive websites.

For the most part, this is about *web services*—server-to-server transmissions of data across the internet, giving rise to web applications that are more adaptable, simply deployed, and interchangeable than in earlier eras. Web services, also called APIs (for Application Programming Interface), let developers tap into incredibly rich, world-class data, functions, and infrastructure, and put them to use powering their own websites. Battelle and O'Reilly also put data-syndication tools like RSS feeds in this same category—essentially, we're talking about formats that set data free, and enable programmers to build new applications by quickly hooking into that data.

Another Web 2.0 innovation is interactive, self-modifying web pages using AJAX ("Asynchronous JavaScript and XML"). JavaScript is a client-side programming language—it runs in the visitor's browser, not on the server of the website. It's a fast, "lightweight" tool that needn't refresh a whole web page to change what it displays. While that may sound prosaic, the effect is huge: AJAX creates fast, dynamic, and interactive web interfaces, where users can click, drag, type, and perform other actions to instantly change a page without waiting for it to reload. Lightweight vector-animation tools, like Flash and its new Microsoft cousin Silverlight, also energize a website with videos, images, text, and navigation that moves, fades, grows, and responds to user's clicks and mouseovers.

The Gap, Banana Republic, and Old Navy were some of the first high-profile ecommerce websites to launch on AJAX technology, back in 2005. It hurts to be first: Their launch was plagued by a 2-week shutdown that the *New York Times* said "turned away thousands of customers and millions of dollars in business." But look at the sites today and you'll see clean, dynamic examples of just how engaging and effective Web 2.0 ecommerce can be. Whether selecting items, choosing their size, and color, or mousing over an array of alternate views, it all generates satisfying and instant responses—displaying availability, swapping images to show views of clothing details, zooming, panning, and more.

Gucci.com is one of the best, most dynamic of Web 2.0 ecommerce interfaces: it delivers animation effects using mostly AJAX, Flash, and Scene7 rich-media images to slide entire categories of products into view, to zoom and rotate the handbags, shoes, jewelry, and apparel, swap colors of product images, and slide selections into the shopping cart.

My impression is that shoppers at these more dynamic, responsive on-line stores experience some of the same feelings researchers have found motivate mall shoppers in the physical world: pleasure, arousal, emotional engagement, and a sense of satisfaction.

Terms to Know

BOT: As in robot, this is a program that runs repeatedly and automatically—to crawl the web, for instance. (The word Bot can also describe a computer that has been taken over by a web virus—see Chapter 7.)

SPIDER: Also known as a "web crawler," this is a program that visits web pages by following the links from one page to another, for the purpose of indexing and (in the case of search engine spiders) ranking them.

XML: Extensible Markup Language—a formatting language that breaks data into fields and puts it into a form that can be used, manipulated, and re-presented anywhere on the web.

More about APIs

Sites with valuable and interesting data often find themselves being screen-scraped: Third-party developers create a bot or spider that routinely visits the target pages, harvests the displayed data, and converts it into reusable form. Perhaps the data is stock quotes, or weather reports, classified ads, or newly updated catalog prices. Although it can create some usefully repurposed data, screen-scraping is an inefficient approach: The program needs to identify and discard all the unwanted code surrounding the desired information. And if the presentation of the page changes significantly, the scraper essentially "breaks" and needs to be reprogrammed before it will return useful stuff.

The cleaner approach, the one that has help launched a revolution, is the API—a system in which an organization lets third-party developers call for and display the data living on its servers. These web services can involve a host of different acronyms depending on their flavor, but the data is typically XML-formatted, and they use the SOAP (Simple Object Access), REST (Representational State Transfer), and/or WSDL (Web Services Description Language) protocols, to make "remote procedure calls" from one entity on the web to another.

You don't need to worry about what all that means. Just understand that APIs are the web services building blocks that let different online applications work together. And while the technology has been around since Web 1.0, it was initially a fairly controlled system: a suite of services opened up to specific business partners in an "integration" project. Today, any web enterprise worth its salt is capable of interacting with key customers, vendors, business partners, freight carriers, etc., through APIs.

But in addition, in recent years we've seen a huge increase in openly available APIs, free and accessible to developers large and small, supported by a self-serve, browser-based interface where developers can easily establish accounts, get documentation, contribute to forums—in other words, a massively scalable ecosystem of custom development that springs up around any useful website that opens itself to it.

APIs are behind many of the data mashups we talked about earlier. Programmable Web, the authority on the subject, catalogs several hundred APIs, and thousands of mashups. For example, Yelp uses the Google Maps API to power its restaurant and other local business reviews—and in turn Yelp opens its own site via web services to developers who might want to mash it up with, say, a mobile local search interface or online ordering service.

Amazon exposes its bestsellers and a slew of other product and customer wish list data to its affiliate partners and the world at large. But beyond that obvious connection to its core business, Amazon also provides APIs to hook into such valuable platforms as its Alexa web traffic database, Amazon WebStore, Flexible Payments platform, storage platform, and "Elastic Compute Cloud."

Robust, useful APIs are also available from YouTube, FaceBook, Yahoo!, Google, MSN, AOL, Adobe—all the big names plus myriad small ones. Today, developers can interact with data from del.icio.us, Amnesty International, Garmin, UPS, federal and state governments, the Library of Congress, you name it. And as we mentioned earlier, working with popular APIs no longer requires the skills of a bona fide programmer, thanks to a host of online API and mashup development tools.

Collective Intelligence

Organizations aren't just poring through the available APIs to find the data to power and enrich their sites—as we mentioned earlier, they're also tapping a formidable army of visitors to supply "user generated" content: profiles, forum and blog entries and comments, ratings and reviews, articles, and software code. Wiki platforms and social media networks harness the energies, personal relationships, and collective intelligence of their communities. In the process, the sites grow and improve under their own power. That's a core example of how Web 2.0 interactivity actually produces a measurable output—the output of collaborative work (or play!).

Feedback Loops

It's not often pointed to as a Web 2.0 characteristic, but the presence of feedback loops between users and website owners is a meaningful part of the big picture. We've had web analytics programs since the dawn of the commercial internet. But in recent years, marketers have focused ever more attention on site experience, abandoned carts, and the like. While incremental performance improvements may come from, say, refining your online advertising keywords, the lion's share of opportunity is to be had by improving site navigation, boosting add-to-cart rates site wide, and optimizing your checkout performance.

Analytics are key to that process, and some dramatic testing tools are on the scene to put any proposed changes to an A/B test with real customers. These tests display alternative versions of your homepage, say, or important navigation elements or "landing pages," and they track which version—or which combination of several variations—delivers the best conversion rate. Such tests are performed in real-time, with variations served up randomly to segments of your audience. Marketers, designers, and GUI architects (the folks behind your Graphical User Interface—your site's "look and feel"), can see the actual conversion-rate lifts produced by particular changes to site content or design.

Sophisticated A/B and multivariate testing tools have been available for some time (and for a cost not negligible), but in my opinion the pair of products most responsible for the wider spread of analytics and usability-testing regimes are both from Google, and both are free: Google Analytics and Google Website Optimizer. Originally Urchin Software, a modestly fee-based software, the platform was bought out, dubbed Google Analytics, and given away for free. Since then, uptake has been jaw-dropping. At the time of this writing, a rumored 250,000 websites are running Google Analytics, including a number of the companies in the *Fortune* 500.

▓ Web Analytics for Web 2.0

The foundation of web analytics has always been visits and page views. Commerce sites, of course, are also interested in sales conversion, average order value, and the performance of their checkout process (also known as a "conversion funnel," on the grounds that of the many people who begin the process, only a fraction continue through each step and complete their order). Community sites may care about visit duration, or number of friend contacts; ad-driven sites care about page impressions of CPC ad clicks.

Web 2.0 has ushered in a whole generation of important behaviors overlooked by the basic analytics package. Here are four Web 2.0 trends forcing us to take a different approach to web stats:

- Real-time, dynamically changing web content, without reloading a page.
- Streaming and interactive media.
- Embedded widgets widely spread across the internet.
- API data called and displayed by sites all across the internet.

Thanks to AJAX, Flash, Silverlight, and other technologies, pages can change radically in response to user behavior, without ever clicking to a new page or refreshing the page view. The same is true for a video or online chat forum, both of which can engage a user's attention for a lengthy session without ever prompting a new page view.

In response, comScore Networks has begun to track the spread of popular widgets—a phenomenon impossible to gauge with a traditional web analytics approach. Likewise, Nielsen NetRatings has abandoned page-views as site-ranking criteria, in favor of length of visit. The rationale is that AJAX, video streaming, and online chat tools all can deliver a long and interactive user session unrecognized by current metrics.

Individual business will need to invest thought and effort into configuring their analytics packages to capture Web 2.0 content—using scripts, for instance, to track particular video or Flash animations and their impact on conversion. Likewise, with the increasing ease and value of deploying A/B split testing, the burden is on the website owner to ensure she captures the relevant data and screens out the noise.

■ Software as a Service (SaaS)

The software industry is using a lot less shrinkwrap these days. Increasingly, software is not an installed product but an on-demand service delivered across the internet in your browser. It's called Software as a Service, or SaaS.

Industry-watcher Phil Wainewright pegs the SaaS industry at roughly $9 billion in revenues, or about 3% to 5% of the global software market. Wainewright, who is a frequent speaker at Computerworld's SaaScon and other events, points out that the line separating "software-as-a-service" from "web applications" is getting blurry indeed.

"It's important to view software-as-a-service in the context of a much broader shift to the web in the way that people interact, both in business and in their social lives. Disconnected or segregated ways of doing things seem increasingly outdated, while collaborative, connected working habits and lifestyles have the look and feel of the future," says Wainewright. "It should be no surprise that software-based services, delivered online and connected into the rich resources of the web, are showing explosive growth right now. Expect them to become the accepted mainstream within the next decade."

Today a business could satisfy virtually all of its enterprise computing needs using SaaS applications. Its website would be hosted by on-demand ecommerce software and be published through a browser interface, integrated with other web services, including email and mailing list-management services, product ratings and reviews, and more. Management and tracking of its online advertising campaigns would be a web app. So would the analytics software. Its product database, inventory, and order data would reside on another on-demand web service. Credit cards would be authorized and settled in real time via an online payment processing service. Reorders from wholesale suppliers would be placed using on-demand supply chain software. Whether using the phone or online chat, the customer-service agents would respond to customer issues through a browser. The sales force would manage its sales forecasting, lead generation, and performance metrics online. Even the enterprise's email communication, document creation, and video conferencing could be performed through web-based, on-demand services.

Here's a small and rather random sampling of popular SaaS options:

- *Web conferencing/collaboration:* WebEx, Citrix Online, Microsoft Live Meeting, Raindance, Acrobat Connect Pro, Zimbra, and many wiki collaboration tools. Also in this category, online chat and IM apps like LivePerson and InstantService.
- *HR and Payroll:* ADP Employease, Paychex, Taleo, Workstream, Successfactors.
- *Customer Relationship Management (CRM) & Fulfillment:* Salesforce, SAP OnDemand, Microsoft Titan, RightNow, Siebel CRM OnDemand, entellium, OrderMotion, etc.
- *Supply Relationship Management (SRM):* SAP eSourcing (formerly Frictionless Commerce), Concur, Ketera, and Rearden Commerce.
- *eCommerce platforms, Content Management Systems, and email marketing software:* This is a huge field with a multitude of players.
- *Accounting & ERP:* NetSuite, Intacct, Intuit QuickBooks OnDemand.
- *Internet Telephony:* Skype, Vonage.

For any website owner, a wealth of powerful, on-demand applications are now available across the internet for integration with your site.

The SaaS phenomenon has two implications for your organization:

- Increasingly, you will be calling across the web to perform software tasks related to your business.
- Any data storage and information processing that you do in the process of serving your customers or business partners is now a candidate for delivery across the web. Envision custom, password-protected websites for your vendors or wholesale customers.

Google and Microsoft's SaaS Battle

If there's any one company that stands to lose when packaged software gives way to web-on-demand, it's Microsoft. But Microsoft has made aggressive strides to web-enable its core Office suite of products and related communications apps. Google, too, sees the opportunity and is wading in.

The first significant web-based software app was Hotmail, launched on July 4, 1996, as a declaration of independence from ISP-based email (i.e., email services delivered by, and bound to, your local internet service provider). Hotmail was bought by Microsoft in 1997, and rechristened Windows Live Hotmail in 2007. At the time of writing this book, it has 380 million users.

Google's answer, Gmail, was launched in 2004 and today has an estimated 50 million users. The appeal of a web-based email system is ever more obvious as we become ever more mobile. Laptop computers now outsell desktop models. We want to send and receive email effortlessly from anywhere, whether we connect to the internet from our office network, home, or a wireless hot spot on the road.

Today, Microsoft and Google are squaring off in the arena of communications and document authoring and sharing. The heart of Microsoft's personal SaaS offerings is its Windows Live and Office Live suite of communications and productivity tools, document sharing, and collaboration apps like LiveMeeting.

Microsoft's longer-range Unified Communication (UC) initiative marries VoIP telephone service, email, audio and video conferencing, voice mail, contacts, calendars, and instant messaging. The angle is to maintain something of the dominance it enjoys in the desktop market after many of these applications move "into the cloud."

Google's answers are Gmail, Google Calendar, Google Talk instant messaging, plus Google Docs, basic web-based word processing, and spreadsheeting that lets users share files and collaborate in real-time. In what is seen as a poke at Microsoft, Google also distributes *Sun's* StarOffice software for free, as a download. And not all of these tools are meant merely to replace the office software on an individual's PC. The Postini email-handling system acquired by Google allows businesses to migrate their entire network's email and spam-filtering operation into the cloud as well.

In addition to Google Apps and Microsoft's personal SaaS offerings, there are some cool smaller players like Goowy Media, who offer a "webtop" alternative to such desktop apps as email, IM, calendar, and contacts.

Whatever of these functions migrate online, from whatever vendor, the stakes are large: Microsoft's business unit, which contains Office, grossed $16.4 billion in 2007.

▓ Rich Media Experiences

With adoption of broadband internet connection and high-speed wireless almost universal now, Web 2.0 sites are able to stream media that rival the richness and entertainment value of TV, radio, film, and game consoles.

Among TV viewers who also have internet access, 55% watch some type of video on their computers, mobile phones, or digital media players (e.g., iPods). As may be expected, video-watching on alternative devices is significantly more popular among younger consumers (66%) than older ones (36%).[1]

The growth of YouTube drew all the headlines, but meanwhile, streaming video and audio, webcasts, and podcasts quickly became part of the fabric of the web, from big enterprise sites to some of the humblest mom and pops.

Red Bull energy drink built its credibility among several wildly different communities, by sponsoring events from pro video gaming to rapping, endurance auto racing to freestyle soccer dribbling, all united by nothing other than their style, high energy, and air of risk. To capture the sound and motion of these events, Red Bull's site is all rich media, Flash, and streaming video. The websites of the NBA, NHL, major league baseball, and other sports leagues also use a lot of rich media, because video and interactivity are crucial to the experience.

Especially if you're in the entertainment world, your website needs to employ rich media. The Dreamworks Animation website is alive with great Flash animation, mouseover navigation, and sound. Dreamworks also interacts with its audience by offering widgets, downloads, animated email signatures, and online games featuring its characters. In contrast, the site of its rival Pixar is dull and static, evoking none of the color, entertainment, and innovation it ought to convey.

Skis.com, Burton Snowboards, Jewelry Television, Buy.com, Lowes, Home Depot, and QVC are all sites that have incorporated video into their online experience.

Meanwhile, powerful advances in 3-D animation have made it possible to create rich, immersive virtual worlds—online environments so realistic and interactive they're capable of engaging millions of users of all ages and nationalities. The same technologies have enabled avatar-based systems that aren't just fun and games: 3-D virtual conferencing, training, and collaborations, to name a few. Interactive text-to-speech avatars from OddCast, which can power real-time online customer service (as well as fun applications like Monk-e-Mail), are another example.

The Mobile Web

The internet is moving off the desktop. For the first time, laptop machines—with their ability to connect wirelessly on the go—are outselling desktop PCs. But growing faster than both of them is the web-enabled phone.

Mobile phones are the fastest-selling consumer electronics in the history of the planet. Worldwide, over a billion cellular telephones are sold each year, and there are over 3 billion of them currently in use. More than 80% of Americans now use them, and about one in eight American households have chucked their landline entirely and gone fully wireless.

The "convergence" debate used to be over whether TV or the PC would be the interactive entertainment device of the future. But it's looking like that crown may belong to web-enabled cell phones.

On average, cell phones are replaced every 18 months, so in addition to their ubiquity and convenience, they're delivering the rapid innovation that will drive much of Web 2.0, and take us right into Web 3.0, whatever that may be.

Today's web-enabled phones combine email and IM, web access, streaming video and audio, wireless connection to other devices, digital camera, and video camera functionality. High-end smart phones also offer PDA-style organizer features, configurable databases, support for mobile video games, substantial MP3, and other file storage capacity, GPS navigation, and more.

North Americans were slower than some corners of the globe to embrace the mobile web, but lately they may be catching up. In a 2007 study by the Online Publishers Association, 71% U.S. respondents have mobile Web access, and 41% actually use it. Seventy-seven percent of Europeans have mobile web access, and 31% are users.[2]

Some Asian markets are even further ahead: notably in Japan, where as many people access the web via their phones as by their PCs—almost 54 million people.[3] It is fruitful to look across to the Pacific to see where our future may be headed. Some Japanese phones, featuring touch-pad interfaces, secured with fingerprint or face-recognition systems, can be used as payment cards: Swiped through store checkout registers, vending machines, and other card readers, they can be used to buy consumer products, train tickets, and more.

Cell phones as mobile payment systems have made major inroads even in Africa—an example of how new technologies can help underdeveloped regions leapfrog entire evolutionary steps: Countries with mature banking industries, broad access to consumer credit, and pervasive landlines have less incentive to adopt innovative new systems built on the wireless web.

▨ The iPhone Effect

In the United States, Apple's iPhone really jumpstarted mobile web access. Though Blackberries, Palms, and a raft of phones had a long head start, the iPhone simply provides a better web-browsing experience than other portables. As I write this, about 4 million iPhones have been sold—strong results, but only a minuscule 2% of smart phones worldwide. So it was big news when Google reported that iPhones topped the list of mobile devices accessing its sites. iPhone users may represent just a small minority of mobile users, but they're already the most numerous mobile web surfers.[4]

One of iPhone's triumphs is that unlike most web phones, it makes it bearable to surf ordinary websites (as opposed to lightweight, scaled-down.mobi ones). Yes, website owners are starting to get on the bandwagon and are building sites designed for the smaller screens of mobile devices—but I'm a bit skeptical of a recent *JupiterResearch* study that claims 40% of website operators have already launched mobile sites, and another 22% plan to do so in the coming year.[5]

"This number is relatively large," states the report, "given that the experience is not yet mature today and likely reflects mobile versions that consist of frames and offer a kludgy user interface."

Whatever the number, we will certainly see more designers building sites optimized for mobile browsing. We'll continue to see both sides meeting in the middle: Portables will continue to improve their ability to render full-size web pages, and more web developers will create stand-alone mobile sites and routinely build "user-agent sniffing" into their sites—so they know whether to display the site normally to web browsers, or to redirect to a mobile version.

Thus far, the industries making the strongest commitments to developing mobile websites have been travel, news, weather, and entertainment companies, as well as the leading web portals and search engines. You can access FaceBook, MySpace, YouTube, Digg, Flickr, and most other social networking apps on the go. Providers of time-sensitive sports news and stock quotes, major banks, and brokers, are also big players. Names like ESPN, Google, Yahoo!, CitySearch, and AccuWeather are usually near the top of mobile website traffic metrics, but there's a multiplicity of other mobile sites, from Maxim to Disney, from NASCAR to NPR, PayPal to FatWallet, which provide good web experiences tailored to phones or PDAs.

CareerBuilder's viral Monk-eMail application that we mentioned in Chapter 1 has also been reengineered for mobile devices, so that animated Monk-eMails can now be sent to handsets through the carriers AT&T, Verizon, and Sprint.

But what about *m-commerce*, or business-to-consumer commerce transacted across mobile devices?

At its mobile phone "entertainment portal" wmtmobile.com, Wal Mart is selling games, ringtones, and wallpapers in partnership with mobile media company PlayPhone. Amazon and eBay enable mobile shopping. At 1800flowers.mobi, 1-800 Flowers makes it possible to order flowers with your phone. "We've all been there," says the company. "It's 3 A.M. and you wake up in a cold sweat, realizing that your anniversary is tomorrow. Or you're on the train to work, and suddenly remember that it's her birthday today. Your worries are over. Now, you can shop for flowers right on your internet-enabled cell phone or mobile device, anytime, anywhere."

With its mobile shopping portal, Barcle lets customers perform price comparisons across 14 million products, sparked either by a keyword or UPC code search. But as testimony to the fact that we're only partway down the road to a mobile web, the Barcle mobile experience shoots visitors off to nonmobile optimized merchant websites to complete a purchase. In a fully mobile web, the device would effortlessly scan the UPC, and the price comparisons and ultimate purchase would take place, end-to-end, on sites optimized for the smaller screen of a mobile device.

When users go mobile, the heavyweight web companies have no intention of being left behind. Google opened Android, its mobile operating system (aka Gphone, aka Open Handset Alliance) as an open standard for

outside developers to create applications and content for mobile devices.
The company further signaled its seriousness about the mobile internet
by bidding in the FCC's January 2008 auction of the wireless spectrum,
aiming to elbow into a market dominated by the major (and notoriously
closed) cell phone carriers. Yahoo! answered Google by opening its mobile
platform to outside developers. With Yahoo! Go, the company serves up
news, stock quotes, email, photo sharing, and more to web-enabled phone
users—hoping to carve out the same portal territory for mobile as it still
maintains for deskbound web surfers.

The Blending of Networks

The line between the internet and the global cellular network is getting fuzzy, too, with cell networks able to perform so many of the same
functions as the web, from text-messaging via SMS to delivering video,
podcasts, and other entertainment. Mobile advertising platform GoLive
Mobile allows marketers to schedule and send campaigns to the cellphones of their subscribers. Mobile campaigns can include text, audio,
video, images, games, and other mobile apps, Flash Lite animations and
videos, XML feed-driven data like stock quotes, and more. Recipients can
make many of the same interactive responses they do on the web: responding to polls, answering trivia questions, paying bills. GoLive also offers a
collection of XML web services to remotely access its mobile platform and
integrate it with web applications.

Verizon's VCast Mobile TV streams television programming to a cell
phone's small screen. Serving the U.S. market is a company called MSGME,
a real-time text-messaging service between merchants and customers.
It's aimed at music labels, bands, media companies and others, even
the smallest of vendors, who could sell songs, ringtones, and games to
phone users. New Line Cinema and Vagrant Records are among the companies using it. Other applications include offering coupons, polls, or an
m-commerce offer.

"Text-to-screen" technology is another interesting riff on the convergence between different types of networks—it harnesses digital billboards
for participants in a public setting at a concert, say, or in Times Square, or
in a bar or coffeehouse, to send chat messages, responses to opinion polls,
sweepstakes, and voting events. Publishers or advertisers can broadcast
a question via radio, television, or print media, and anyone with a cell
phone can respond via SMS.

The mobile internet landscape is growing fast and changing fast, and
it's offering no clear road map for companies wanting to explore it. The

marketplace is fragmented, dominated by a few national cellular carriers each guarding their proprietary networks—with lots of small specialist companies popping up to help publishers and advertisers make sense of it all. It's a time of uncertainty and opportunity—and to many, it feels a little like the early days of the commercial internet.

4 ▪ ▪ ▪

Case Studies: Rapidly Changing Online Landscapes

The internet is the very embodiment of *disruptive technology*—a term coined by Harvard Business School professor Clayton Christensen, to describe any innovation that upsets the old order. What cars did for the horse-and-buggy, the web is doing, in varying degrees, for everything from newspapers to postage stamps, *TV Guide* to travel agents, packaged CDs to packaged software.

Web 2.0 continues to radically remake existing industries—and also to launch new ones from scratch.

Let's take a look at four areas where the innovations of Web 2.0 are rapidly changing the landscape:

- Entertainment
- Advertising
- eCommerce
- Search

▦ Online Entertainment

"Within 10 years, the consumption of anything we think of as media today—whether it is print, TV or the Internet—will in fact be delivered over IP and will all be digital," says Microsoft CEO, Steve Ballmer.[1] "Everything will be delivered digitally."

While media execs are skeptical of Ballmer's all-or-nothing prediction, the TV, film, music, radio, and games industries have already been radically remade by Web 2.0. Broadcast television has been disconnected from its ads and its real-time schedule, thanks to TiVo. Much of the same programming, and myriad other videos, professional and amateur, are available at YouTube. Fiercely competing delivery platforms—video, radio, and games on cable and satellite networks, the web, game consoles, portable video players, iPod music, and video—are all chasing ever-shorter attention spans.

The Year the Music Industry Broke

The internet has "unbundled" the entertainment business. Shows are untethered from their ads, songs untethered from their albums. Say goodbye to the compact disk. CD album sales are plunging about 15% a year. But with surging paid downloads or subscriptions from iTunes, Rhapsody, and others, the music industry is primed to start growing again with what looks like a sustainable financial model for Web 2.0 music sales. Getting there wasn't pretty—remember the RIAA's 20,000 illegal-downloading lawsuits targeting teenagers, grandmas, and everyone in-between, in the days before Napster was shut down? It took Apple's innovation to pull the record companies to the table.

MTV dubbed 2007 "the year the music industry broke." One theme raised by MTV sounds like an echo of findings in Chris Anderson's *The Long Tail*. Gone are the days of big hit albums for the masses. We're now in the age of niche successes for countless niches. We cherry-pick favorite tracks for 99 cents rather than being force-fed a whole album. As MTV sees it, our attention flits between ever more distractions:

> *Even if you were the most famous rapper on the planet or the winner of "American Idol," your album might have gotten lost in the shuffle as music fans spent their time downloading free albums from bands like Radiohead, watching the new "Chocolate Rain" viral clip, scouring gossip sites for news on Britney's latest antics, dialing up Soulja Boy ringtones, watching bootleg clips on YouTube, buying the latest J. Lo fragrance or trying on some of Gwen's L.A.M.B. clothes.[2]*

The YouTube Phenomenon

It's not just the music scene. Online video has taken over Americans' leisure time in a big way. Some 86% of high speed internet users watch streaming video at least once a month.[3] The movement started at the grass roots: millions of home movies, amateur videos, and recorded TV clips uploaded at YouTube and other video sites, whose traffic doubled in 2007.[4]

The entertainment companies came along belatedly and grudgingly, and even now they lack a clear model for monetizing their video property. Barry Diller's IAC and Rupert Murdoch's News Corp are leading the rest of the entertainment industry, which Diller derides as "temporarily prehistoric" when it comes to online efforts.

But the transformation is well underway: You can watch clips on YouTube, MetaCafe, or at broadcaster sites like ComedyCentral, or you can have video podcasts sent to our PC, phone, or iPod. Comcast's Fancast service joined a field of companies offering online streaming TV programming, games, and other multimedia streams. AOL's "In2TV" service, Hulu.com, Joost, BitTorrent, and Yahoo! TV are just a few of the other players.

Each new entertainment success spawns a multitude of specialty niches. Special-interest YouTube imitators now include ShoeTube, devoted to footwear, JewTube for Jewish videos, and GodTube, a Christian programming venue, which according to comScore, recently ranked as the fastest-growing site on the web!

In a cool bit of technology convergence, Yahoo! TV enables its users to program their TiVos remotely via the web. Fancast, too, announced plans to let its members program their DVRs online.

We are still witnessing the birth pains of entertainment 2.0. A bitter and protracted writers' strike over online rights and royalties, and emerging tech standards for digital video from mobile devices merely muddies the immediate future—but the longer term future is clear: People will consume their video and other media in ever-smaller chunks, on their own schedule, and on the device of their choosing.

Market researcher Jack Plunkett sums it up nicely:

Consumers, especially consumers in younger demographics, now demand more and more control over what they watch, read and listen to ... The implications of these changes are staggering. The business models upon which most entertainment companies have traditionally run are becoming obsolete.[5]

The Incredible Shrinking Attention Span

Naysayers used to write off the internet as an entertainment platform mainly because sitting at the PC was never going to be as comfortable as the couch. But two developments combined to make the web the fastest-growing entertainment platform:

- Web-enabled portable music and video devices, including cell phones and iPods.
- Viewing habits shift to shorter-form video.

The latter point marks a major cultural shift. Movies, books, articles, even commercials, are getting steadily shorter. Where our parents and grandparents gladly sat through 3-hour epic films and read 600-page novels, today's media consumers want their entertainment in bite-sized pieces: a couple of minutes of music video, a segment on Comedy Central, sports or news highlights rather than the entire broadcast, and amateur productions to satisfy any interest, funny bone, or libido.

The average YouTube video is under 3 minutes long. Some 75% of all digital video streamers have watched brief news, sports, and comedy clips, and about two-thirds have watched short amateur videos. But only 26% have watched full-length TV shows—and a paltry 15% have streamed a full-length movie.[6]

Despite the explosion of shorter-form entertainments, no one is predicting the demise of feature-length movies and other programming.

DVDs will likely meet the same fate as CDs, but before that happens Netflix aims to be out in front of the TV and movie download business. The company has earmarked $40 million to pursue digital download initiatives in 2008. Blockbuster, HBO, and others have rolled out their own download services. For its part, Netflix is betting that not the computer, but smart televisions hooked into the broadband internet, will be the delivery platform of the future.

"The big opportunity for Netflix online video arrives when we can deliver content to the television without requiring a laptop or a media center PC as an intermediary device," said Netflix CEO, Reed Hastings.[7] "We are working hard with various partners to make this a reality in 2008."

Online Gaming

The video game business now rivals DVD sales and rental in terms of total sales, and some industry professionals predict it will, for the first time, eclipse the size of the music industry. Online games, already a $4 billion business, will grow an estimated 25% a year to reach $11.8 billion by 2011, says Boston-based Strategy Analytics.[8]

"The main driver for sustained growth in the online games market will be the continued uptake of broadband services around the world," adds David Mercer, principal analyst at the research firm.

That would account for fully a third of the entire video game market size by that time. Chief source of the online growth will be the tens of millions playing Massively Multiplayer Online Games (MMOGs) like World of Warcraft, RuneScape, SecondLife, and other role-playing and sim games. The web is uniquely suited as a delivery platform for multiplayer games. The global, multiplayer nature of these virtual worlds makes today's gamers notably social and interactive, helping shuck off the old couch-potato gamer stereotype.

- World of Warcraft has 8.5 million subscribers (about half in the West, and half in Asia).
- Habbo Hotel has 7.5 million active users.
- RuneScape has 5 million active users, of which about 1 million are paid subscribers.
- Club Penguin, a social environment for young kids, has 4 million active users.
- Webkinz, also for kids, has 3.8 million active users.
- Second Life has about 14 million residents (but fewer than 10% qualify as active, having logged in within the past two months).

Another huge transformation for the gaming world is referred to as "electronic sell-through and digital distribution" of both PC and console games—in other words, buying and downloading games across the web rather than buying shrink-wrapped games from a retail store.

While most publishers are working on paid download models, Electronic Arts is experimenting with free downloads of games like FIFA Soccer and its Battlefield series. This business model depends exclusively on revenue from in-game advertising and player "micropayments"—small fees that players choose to pay to buy high-end weapons, equipment, custom clothing, or to soup-up the skills, speed, or agility of their character.[9] Products like Microsoft's Xbox Live bridges the gap between console gaming and online gaming, allowing gamers to play games in real time with users across the internet.

There's a huge and growing market for so-called "casual games," such as card games, puzzles, word games, arcade and casino-style games, board games, and the like. Casual games are easily learned, they don't require much hand-eye coordination or mastering complicated game platforms, and they don't soak up the hundreds of hours hard-core gamers devote to their multilevel, multiplayer games.

Available as free real-time streams, or quick and inexpensive downloads, casual games are perfect for the internet—and they have very quickly become gaming's biggest segment.

The Casual Games Association claims 150 million people play free, casual games online, outpacing game consoles, first-person shooter games, and massively multiplayer games. Girls and women make up 74% of the casual gaming market. That's a demographic long sought after by the industry, whose bread-and-butter has until now been young males.

We've also witnessed a flood of online games for phones, iPods, and portable game consoles. As with casual gaming, handheld owners are a more gender-balanced lot. Nielsen reported that while active gamers average about 14 hours a week on their consoles, surprisingly they also play as much as 17 hours a week on handhelds. Some 24% of active gamers also play games on their cell phones.[10]

▓ Online Advertising

After cratering with the burst of the internet bubble, then perking up only modestly in the several months after 9/11, online ad spending is today a $20 billion a year business in the United States alone. In recent years, it has soared a jaw-dropping 30% a year.

What happened—and what's coming next?

Paid Search

Since 2003, the growth chart of the online advertising market has been climbing in a hockey-stick pattern, thanks mostly to the explosion of cost-per-click text ads on the major search-engines. Meanwhile, banner advertising has, for over a decade, wandered through periods of hype, discredit, and rehabilitation.

The paid search business started from scratch in 1998 with the founding by Bill Gross of GoTo, the world's first paid-click arbitrageur. Today, creaky, gray-haired emarketers like me remember those days with fondness, hitching up our suspenders and getting misty-eyed with the memory of one-penny clicks.

The full evolution of search advertising is told in gripping detail by John Battelle in *The Search*. But the Cliff Notes version is this: GoTo changed its name to Overture in 2001, and grew by syndicating its paid ad listings on major search engines MSN and Yahoo!. Google got in on the action in 2000 by launching its Google AdWords platform, which garners more than half of all searches today and the lion's share of search-advertising dollars.

Yahoo!, no longer content with a mere online advertising rev-share model, snapped up Overture in 2003 for $1.7 billion. In 2005 MSN and Ask each launched their own ad-serving platforms, and in 2007, AOL followed suit. Today, every organization with a vowel in its name seems to offer its own cost-per-click ad platform.

Paid search in particular, and online search in general, has grown due to:

- Adoption by more advertisers.
- Migration of ad budgets from offline to online media.
- Increasing "inventory" of users, searches, page-views, and clicks.
- Click-price inflation.
- Development of new online media and portable devices.

Shifting Dollars

In 2001, when the needle started to move, 29% of advertisers migrated some of their marketing online. Since then, new advertisers have continued to come into the fold, and existing ones have upped their online ad spending—in some cases at the expense of traditional media budgets. In 2006, essentially all the $4 billion growth in online advertising came at the expense of offline media.[11]

When it comes to spending, global internet advertising has already surpassed billboard advertising and radio advertising. By 2010 it is expected to climb past magazines to become the third-biggest ad medium, after television and newspapers.

By migrating more ad dollars to the web, marketers are following two metrics, ROI (return on investment), and eyeballs (number of viewers). For direct marketers, although the gap is tightening fast, online advertising still demonstrates advantages in cost-per-acquisition.

Internet ad spending by American Express, for example, jumped by 180%, while its total ad spending dropped by 13.1%.

Increasing Inventory

Growth in web usership has slowed due to high rates of penetration worldwide, but it does continue to grow, and people are also spending more of their work hours and leisure time online either at computers or on web-enabled phones and portables. More users, more search queries, more page-views, and more clicks all add up to more revenue for the sellers of online advertising.

Click-price Inflation

Unfortunately for online marketers, the growth of inventory appears to be slowing, while migration of advertising dollars still has a long, long way to go. Recently, the web represented 25% of our total media consumption—but a mere 6% of total ad spending. All things being equal, this imbalance between media consumption and media ad spending is bound to change. If the web is where all the customers are, the advertising dollars will follow them there.

Indeed, eMarketer projects that online advertising will more than double as a percentage of total media, rising to slightly over a 12% share in 2010.

That means more competition for available clicks, and it's not the only year-over-year trend looking ugly for your online ROI. According to a recent DoubleClick Performics study[12] of 50 large and well-managed paid search campaigns:

1. The average cost-per-click (CPC) climbed 55%.
2. Orders grew 38%—in other words, slower than click costs.
3. Sales dollars grew even less, at 28%.
4. The growth of search queries, across all search engines, slowed to 11%.
5. ROI fell 16%.

Most direct marketers will still tell you that their online advertising—especially paid search and comparative shopping platforms—delivers some of the highest-ROI and most incremental (new-to-file) customers.

But what disproportionate ROI has existed in paid search is starting to slip away. As it approaches a more efficient market, as more advertisers flock to the medium, and as the ad platforms continue to eliminate practical obstacles (like the difficulty of building, managing, and scaling campaigns), bid prices will keep climbing and ROIs will sink, until the medium is pretty comparable to other DM alternatives.

The Interactive Advertising Bureau predicted U.S. online advertising to grow at 22% in 2008, boosted in part by the Olympic Games and the U.S. Presidential election, before the growth rate tails off into the mid to low teens through 2011. And while that growth rate may be flattening, the industry still dwarfs the gross national product of many a third world nation—an estimated $36.5 billion by 2011.

Display Advertising

Banner ads couldn't live up to the early promise of "monetizing the eyeballs" of many an overhyped Web 1.0 site. Then, online display advertising became overshadowed by the explosion of successful paid-search platforms. The pay-for-performance model, the low minimum investment and the clear, trackable ROI, made paid search everything that banner ads were not. But today online display advertising still dwarfs paid search, and many marketers are more excited about the medium than ever.

Paid search appeals mostly to direct marketers. Banner ads, with their flashier visuals, have been the promise of brand marketers eager to introduce a product, bolster their brand image and recognition, or generate buzz for a movie or new car. The biggest online display advertisers really run the gamut: Netflix, eBay, the big cell phone carriers, investment firms like Fidelity and eTrade, Monster.com and other job sites, mortgage companies. But the real sea change has been the many smaller companies getting into the game.

Display advertising is getting more respect, for a number of reasons:

- New self-service CPC ad-serving platforms.
- New rich-media and video ads.
- Rapidly-growing social networks and other user-created pages.
- Realization that banner ads and search ads work in concert.

First, by allowing paid search advertisers to create display ads of various shapes and sizes and syndicate them across their Content Networks, the big engines created a new ecosystem where small marketers could get new (although not usually very lucrative) exposure to mainstream and niche sites—from Popular Mechanics or Web MD to a humble blog. Ad platforms like Quigo, AdBrite, and others provided similar do-it-yourself access to inventory on sites as diverse as CNN, Entertainment Weekly, CareerBuilder, BoingBoing, Drudge Report, and more. Advertisers have responded to better targeting options, lower minimum buys, and the cost-per-click rather than cost-per-impression business model.

Second, advertisers have a lot of more interactive and rich-media choices to work with than the animated gifs of yore. Ads with streaming audio and video, ads with Flash animation, sliders, and other ads, which move into the screen as a layer on top of content, ads featuring interactive games. The bottom line: although many of us may view them as annoying, dynamic interactive ads are better at getting customer attention and response.

Third, most of the largest growth stories of Web 2.0 have been social networks of one sort or another. Participants at FaceBook, MySpace,
and LinkedIn spend a lot of time messaging (or poking) each other and
installing and playing with widgets. Their profile pages don't offer con-
sistent content that makes it easy to serve up relevant "contextually targeted" ads. The searches they perform don't have obvious commercial
intent (we'll get to the troubled early history of Social Advertising in a
few pages). The rapid growth of these social-media pages, blogs, wikis, and
other user-created content has created millions of new pages in need of a
business model. And banner advertisers, especially in the entertainment
business, are attracted to the demographic.

Finally, it has become clear that judging an ad medium as either
brand marketing or direct marketing doesn't tell the full story. Previously, search engine ads were seen as producing a great ROI solely on
their own. But advertisers have begun to recognize that most purchases
are a multistep process, and brand advertising is a key part of guiding
general, nonbrand searchers onto a specific path to purchase.

A 2006 study of online retailers found that 25% of customers clicked on
more than one ad before buying.[13] Of these, the highest-converting customers were those who first performed a generic, nonbrand search, and
then, later, returned with a specific brand-name search. Such searchers
were *seven times more likely to convert* than a customer using only nonbrand
searches.

Brand-oriented display ads can be served up in response to general
searches, or displayed on relevant pages, or in front of relevant audiences.
The effect is to help the general-interest searcher to refine his or her shopping process, so that an initial search for "safest minivan" might over time
elicit a second search for "Honda," then a later one for "Honda Odyssey."
With the right media-buying strategy, display ads create the brand awareness that drives shopping searches, and influence which search ads get
clicked. Giving all the credit to the final click fails to acknowledge the important role played by display ads and other pieces of the marketing mix.

The big search engines are certainly convinced there's synergy between the two media, and have gone on a multibillion-dollar buying
spree: Google bought DoubleClick, Yahoo! bought Right Media, Microsoft
bought aQuantive, and AOL bought Tacoda. Display ads will inspire search
clicks—and thanks to the marriage between search engines and display
ad networks, these companies will get a piece of both pies.

Social Advertising

The enormous growth of Facebook, Myspace, YouTube, and their ilk has
many people predicting a boom in social media advertising. But before

it comes to pass, expect to see a lot of false starts. We've already seen some doozies.

Facebook walked into a privacy fiasco when it went too far connecting ads to the social graph, and had to scrap the most controversial part of the program—the "Beacon" feature that tracked users' purchases on other, non-Facebook sites, and reported them to their friend network as part of the member News Feed.

Beacon gave Facebook a big black eye over privacy concerns and the many awkward scenarios to which the cookie-driven ad strategy gave rise: surprise gifts being spoiled, embarrassing video rentals being revealed. The bad press was relentless, tens of thousands of users joined a Move.org petition drive, and others readied an FTC complaint against the company before Facebook pulled the plug.

Privacy blowups notwithstanding, ad spending on social networking sites is expected to soar to $3.63-billion globally by 2011, according to eMarketer—an almost threefold increase.[14]

Facebook offers a well-designed, self-service text ad platform that gives advertisers simply incredible targeting options with a few mouse clicks. Want to reach fans of Jack Johnson? Or single Christian men aged 30 to 40? Graduates from Ivy League schools, or employees of Microsoft, or all Facebook members in Mexico? No problem.

Well, maybe one problem: Even with its millions of members, when you start paring down the audience into segments like these, the numbers get underwhelming pretty quickly. And the targeting criteria are a far cry from paid search, where someone searching for an item is, presumably, interested in buying it. In contrast, when a new member joins a social network, she names a handful of favorite books, movies, bands, and other interests on her profile. To assume these make her a good candidate for ads targeting her interest is a bit of a stretch.

MySpace now calls itself the "world's largest ad targeting platform," and its Google-powered HyperTargeting service offers advertisers the ability to aim its pitches at MySpace members around ten product categories including music, sports, movies, and games, each with subcategories down to specific teams, bands, and the like. Early adopters have been big brand marketers like Taco Bell, Procter & Gamble, Ford, Toyota, McDonald's, and Wendy's. But expect some bumps on the road to multibillion-dollar social ad spending. Google, which put its neck out by guaranteeing a payout to MySpace, initially reported disappointing social-media ad revenues: "We have found that social networks are not monetizing as well as we were expecting," said George Reyes, Google's chief financial officer.

In addition to advertising directly with the social sites, a new avenue for reaching people in social networks is widget advertising. Advertising.com launched a "Widgnet" advertising program that pairs advertiser messages with the popular miniapplications that social networkers can plug-and-play on their profile pages.

Many open questions still hover around social media advertising. For one, it's creepy. People have become comfortable airing personal information with total strangers in a globally accessible forum. But they're still not fully comfortable with that same information about likes and dislikes, recent purchases and friendships to be targeted for direct marketing of products, or used to pitch their friends.

In my own experience with Facebook, few of the ads I've seen are targeted to my interests, groups, or demographic—they're just the random run-of-site ads ranging from acne medications to the University of Phoenix MBA.

Still, there's no question the audience is there: eMarketer reported 70% of online teens and 37% of online adults in the United States already participate in social networking, and the numbers continue to grow. The researcher projects that by 2011 social networking will involve one-half of online adults and 84% of online teens.[15]

Marketers are definitely starting to experiment with social network advertising, with $1.6 billion projected to be spent by U.S. firms in 2008. Worldwide, online social network ad spending is expected to approach $2.2 billion. MySpace, with more than twice the traffic of Facebook, should sell $525 million worth of advertising in 2008, according to eMarketer. Facebook is expected to bring in $140 million.

Behavioral Targeting

While the social networks are rolling out new approaches to targeting, the big display advertising platforms are still several steps ahead of them. Most of the direct-response money seems still to be made in paid search, but literally scores of new advertising networks have emerged, competing for that growing online ad budget. The players include Advertising.com, Valueclick, Adbrite, TribalFusion, Casale Media, 24/7 RealMedia, and more.

The prevailing financial models are:

- Cost-per-click (CPC)
- Cost-per-acquisition (CPA)
- Cost-per-thousand impressions (CPM)

Some advertising and targeting options include:

- Paid search (display ads relevant to a search query)
- Contextual advertising (display ads relevant to the context of a page)
- Geo-targeting (customize ads based on the users' location)

- Site targeting (display ads only on selected sites within a larger ad network)
- Category targeting (e.g., display ads on all food and nutrition sites)
- Connection speed targeting (display only to users with fast connections)
- Language targeting
- At-home versus at-work
- Dayparting (schedule ads to run only at particular times of the day)
- Remarketing (display ads only to visitors who previously visited your site)
- Behavioral targeting (display ads based on previous sites user visited or links user clicked on, etc.)

Two of the most interesting targeting options offered by these platforms are *behavioral targeting* and *remarketing.*

Behavioral targeting, or BT, uses cookies to track a web user's past behaviors and predict which advertising he will best respond to. Years ago, the early practitioners of behavioral targeting were the notorious adware operators, like Gator, who installed their software deviously, and plagued user machines with unwanted popup ads.

In the years since, the industry has radically cleaned up its act and adopted clear privacy and ethics rules. More important, they've gone to a user-friendly delivery platform, working in the background on a huge network of the web's most visited sites—reaching around 80% of all U.S. web users.

The ad networks have built extensive database relationships between websites, products, and user demographics. They may know that a male visitor to L.L. Bean correlates well to a prospective customer at Cabela's. A woman visitor to L.L. Bean may correlate better to J.Jill. The sophistication of today's BT goes well beyond this example, into particular search queries and browsing behaviors.

eMarketer forecasts that spending on behavioral targeting will be $3.8 billion by 2011. Advertising.com, ValueClick, TribalFusion, 24/7 Realmedia, and a raft of other advertising networks can now offer some flavor of behavioral targeting.[16]

Yahoo! SmartAds is a behavioral targeting approach that serves customized display ads based on user's age, gender, geographical location, or browsing history. In launch testing, SmartAds generated $2\times$ to $3\times$ increases in click rates compared to displaying static, uncustomized ads to the same demographics.

Remarketing is to my mind one of the most attractive opportunities in behavioral targeting. First, you make a deal with a big online network, say Advertising.com, Acerno, or Tacoda for instance. Then, visitors to your website receive a cookie or tracking pixel from the ad network; if they leave your site without buying anything, the ad network is primed to recognize them should they visit any of the sites in its advertising network. Since, as we said, these ad networks reach some 80% of web surfers, eventually, cookied users do reemerge, whether at CNN, the *Chicago Tribune*, About.com, or wherever.

That's when the ad networks serve up your banner ads, which—since the person is one of your past visitors—should enjoy high brand recognition. In my experience, remarketing ads provide about a 3% to 6% lift to your overall site conversion rate. They also have the benefit of burnishing your brand image, since your ads seem to appear all over the internet. Regardless of your size, they make you seem a ubiquitous advertiser, at least in the eyes of your own past visitors.

So on the one hand, they're really effective. On the other hand, they *should* be. After all, you've selected a terrifically targeted group—people who've visited your website, perhaps in response to your advertising, perhaps because they have bought from you in the past. So you're commissioning a third party to bring them back to your store with some additional ads.

And with BT, as with any of the emerging ad-targeting platforms, you really have to weigh the revenue opportunity against the creepiness factor.

Ad networks offering behavioral targeted ads have taken some pains to respect privacy and ensure that not *all* of a web surfer's browsing behavior becomes fair game for displaying ads. Consider, for instance, the person who discreetly researches a sensitive medical condition, or one who secretly consumes online pornography. If "relevant" ads were to start appearing elsewhere on the web—for that user and others in his household who shared the computer—it could be pretty troubling.

Thanks to paid search and the associated content networks, customers are getting pretty sophisticated about identifying why, when, and how ads are being targeted at them. The Facebook firestorm demonstrated just how a poorly conceived ad technology could backfire.

Video and Audio

Online video has shown incredible power to grab and hold audiences, and to generate a sprawling social energy of new content creation, rating, tagging, and commenting. Over half the U.S. population is watching online video,[17] and advertisers are eager to get into the game. In 2007, online video ad spending jumped 89% over the previous year, to $775 million.

The online media industry is still just beginning to see what advertising formats catch on with advertisers and gain acceptance from viewers. The standard and ubiquitous unit is the preroll ad that plays before the chosen video loads. While prerolls do indeed get watched, they're generally unloved. A survey by Burst Media found that 75% of online video-watchers find in-video ads "intrusive."[18] That percentage closely matches the number of television viewers who channel-surf, chat, or fetch a snack during TV commercials. So advertisers are looking for more interactive, opt-in ads that viewers would view more positively. Meanwhile, there's been a migration away from 30-second toward 15-second prerolls as a less intrusive interruption of the in-stream video.

To be part of the surging popularity of online video, most businesses have four avenues:

- Produce video to enrich your website and/or promotional emails
- Enable video-sharing on your website to engage your customers in an online community
- Post video (containing your company name and domain name) on YouTube and other social media sites
- Advertise on video platforms, either in video, display, or text ad formats

Many Web 2.0 media agencies exist to help companies generate video content, distribute it, or advertise in online rich-media environments. Now small local businesses can get into the game, too—for $1,000, local-search player SuperPages will come onsite to a local business, shoot documentary-style 30- or 60-second spots, then run them on Super-Pages.com.

The Associated Press distributes its video programming to its affiliated local news stations and other websites, embedded in the AP's video player widget. Local sites can share in the revenue of online video ads, and AP provides them with browser-based tools to let them upload their own locally produced video content—along with local advertising.

You can advertise on YouTube by running promoted videos, placing display ads or video ads, or having your ad message delivered in-video. If you generate a lot of video content and have deeper pockets, you can sponsor contests or build a "Brand Channel" around your offerings.

YouTube, VideoEgg, Scan Scout, and others offer a variety of video advertising units, including the venerable preroll. One new approach is video overlay, where an advertiser's ad message is touted on a "ticker" on the outside of the media player interface; when clicked, it pauses the original video and telescopes the ad into the screen.

The other approach to monetizing all that streaming video is not so much to interrupt it but simply to surround it with billboards: banners and text advertising. That sounds very Web 1.0, but today the players are employing some sort of content matching, as with the content networks of the big three search engines, to try to pair each video with relevant ads based on the topic of the video.

Companies like Adap.tv, Digitalsmiths, Pluggd, and others have sprung up with speech- and video-recognition technologies and algorithms to better identify the content of a video, and match it dynamically with closely targeted ad content.

If there really are affinities between video-watching and consumer behavior, advertisers will eventually want to be there. Right now, online video is the province of the major brand advertisers and entertainment media. But there are already real world examples that work for direct marketers, such as accompanying an online cooking video with ads for cookbooks or kitchen gear.

In-Game Advertising

Video game advertising has been the area of a lot of hype and speculation of late, with analysts estimating $1 billion ad revenues by 2010 or so. Much of that would be for brand-placement within the graphical environment of bestselling console games. But there are a host of other advertising opportunities, including display ads, and video on the online casual games platforms.

But even some highly placed industry execs are wary of such forecasts, recognizing that the long-term future of any advertising-supported media depends on synergy between advertiser and audience. As Sony CEO Harold Stringer rather candidly put it, "Young people don't like advertising very much."[19]

We've all heard about the companies establishing their virtual islands on Second Life. Reuters operates a full-fledged SL news agency. Coca Cola, Sears, Dell Computer, Reebok, Coldwell Banker, Calvin Klein, and scores of other brands are there. But it's unclear what they're getting out of it. Few of these virtual destinations get more than a few thousand visitors a week.[20]

As with social networks, the key to participating as a company is first to understand and participate as a person. If there's a good cultural fit, and your organization can appeal to and reach a core community of customers and evangelists, go for it. But these environments, despite the millions of residents, are not mass-marketing media. At the time of writing this book, Second Life boasted around 14 million residents, but only 1.3 million had logged in within the past two months, which suggests that some 90% of their claimed usership is, essentially, inactive. And only a relative handful can be at the same place at the same time. Essentially, MMOGs are person-to-person, real-time events. It seems most companies should view their participation as a learning experience and not buy into too much hype.

"It seems people are worried the bubble is about to pop," writes Joey Seiler of VirtualWorldsNews.com. "2008 is a year to prove virtual worlds have value, and convince managers, enterprise-level organizations, and media brands that there are highly specific and necessary use cases. Otherwise the backlash is coming."[21]

Mobile Advertising

Advertising on web-enabled phones, Blackberries, and other PDAs is a field that's ripe for growth. So far, advertisers have shown little appetite for mobile video advertising—just 1% of advertisers, and 3% of agencies surveyed in a 2007 *JupiterResearch* study[22] had bought ads packaged for mobile video, but that is set to change quickly.

The killer app for mobile devices is local search. eMarketer sees mobile internet users more than doubling, to 64.8 million in 2011, and nearly all of them—some 55.8 million—will be using mobile search. Mobile search ad revenues, meanwhile, are seen going from almost nothing to over $700 million by 2011. Search would make up 15% of a total mobile advertising market of some $4.7 billion.[23]

And what would make up the other 85%?

"More than a dozen Fortune 100 companies are advertising on mobile, with the heaviest representation being among media companies advertising websites, TV shows, movies and books," said Will Hodgman, president and CEO of mobile advertising analytics firm M:Metrics. "The automotive, travel and leisure and financial services industries are also making investments into the mobile medium. It's not just games and ringtones—it's everything from iced coffee to auto insurance. Mobile is showing a speed of adoption that we are only now seeing in the internet."

eCommerce (Business-to-Consumer Product Retailing)

Lauren Freedman is president of the e-tailing group, an ecommerce retailing research firm, and consultant to online merchants. Over many years, Freedman and her company have worked with Fortune 500 firms and startups, and brands like Crate & Barrel, J. Jill, Orvis, Lowe's, Toys R Us, Sears, Circuit City, and many others. The e-tailing group's merchant surveys, mystery shopping work, and other research gives them some unique insight into the online shopping experience, and where leading merchants are going with their online strategies.

Freedman finds that retailers, though keen to identify technologies that will boost performance of their online stores, are naturally driven by return on investment.

"Does it deliver from an ecommerce perspective? It's still early yet for some of these things. Merchants are looking for essential things that are proven to work. Rich media images are popular with shoppers, but there is a cost associated with it for the merchant, especially one with a high SKU count." In this case, Freedman says, merchants might introduce richer Web 2.0 features like video, or image zoom for its most popular products, mindful of the 80–20 rule. "Smart merchants are very ROI-centric. It has to deliver a return."[24]

It also pays to remember why people like shopping online in the first place: A holiday season Shop.org survey[25] found it was mostly about convenience and selection, rather than about advanced features. Top reasons to avoid the malls and shop online:

- Ability to shop at any time of day (58.5%)
- Ability to avoid the crowds (43.8%)
- Convenience of online shopping (38.7%)
- Ability to compare prices online (36.2%)
- Items are easier to find online than in stores (29.9%)

Interactive Shopping Wizards

As for the suitability of Web 2.0 shopping tools, Freedman suggests, "It's all about fit for category and fit for brand." If you're doing business in consumer electronics, a product comparison tool will be a must. But in other categories it would be irrelevant.

A good example is the product-selection wizards at Sears.com: The interactive, Flash-driven "Kitchen Advisor" that lets customers dynamically search for and compare kitchen appliances; with the Sears 3-D kitchen tool, powered by MyVirtualModel, shoppers can mix, match, and preview their choice of kitchen layouts, appliances, cabinet styles, and color schemes.

BlueNile's trademarked "Build Your Own Ring" functionality is another great marriage (sorry, I couldn't resist!) between Web 2.0 technology and the core challenge a ring-shopper needs to solve: how to combine gemstone, size, and cut with ring material, style, and size—all in a budget, from a universe of choices that might range from $99 to $1 million. Since BlueNile is a category killer, its onsite search engine is of little help to focus a shopping experience: A search for "diamond ring" will yield hundreds of results, each of which can be paired with thousands of stones. But BlueNile's step-by-step "Build Your Own Ring" process guides customers through each refinement, with the ability to envision the tradeoffs made with each selection.

Home Depot's "Grill Finder" is another helpful tool, and one that was reported to have lifted conversion rates 50% when used; eBags "Build Your Own Bag" is another example. A related concept is "purpose-driven navigation." Done right, interactive shopping tools simplify complex products, and they also entertain and engage the shopper.

In a 2007 customer satisfaction survey performed by *ForeSee Results* among shoppers at the 100 biggest online retailers, websites were much more likely to be gauged on down-to-earth measures like product availability and ease of navigation than they were on Web 2.0 enhancements.[26] Nevertheless, these top 25% of customer-pleasing sites do use an array of cutting-edge features. The most universally adopted by merchants and praised by shoppers: customer ratings and reviews.

Another survey,[27] asking U.S. online retailers what customer-service improvements they had made to their sites in anticipation of the holiday season, was dominated by what I'd consider Web 1.0 basics: faster checkout, online order tracking, stored shipping and billing info, and online inventory status checking. But a number of Web 2.0 enhancements made the list, including:

Customer reviews 25%
Product videos 13%
Live chat 10%

Ratings and Reviews

On the web today, and in life at large, we consumers are cynical, jaded, and intuitively able to see through BS. Bombarded with an estimated 5,000 advertising messages a day, we're now masters at tuning them out, and when we do pay any attention, we're increasingly skilled at separating the marketing hype from reality. And one of the key ways we do that now is word-of-mouth (WOM) recommendations from other consumers. For almost eight out of ten customers in a recent Nielsen survey, WOM is a trusted form of product communication, ranking higher than any other. At 61%, "consumer opinions posted online" are another top influencer. According to Nielsen, here's how all sources stacked up in terms of trustworthiness:

Recommendations from consumers	78%
Newspapers	63%
Consumer opinions posted online	61%
Brand websites	60%
Television	56%
Magazines	56%
Radio	54%
Brand sponsorships	49%
Email	49%
Ads before movies	38%
Search engine ads	34%
Online banner ads	26%
Text ads on mobile phones	18%

Some 65% of all online shoppers are what the e-tailing group calls Social Researchers—people whose shopping decisions are mostly influenced by word-of-mouth recommendations and product reviews from people like themselves.

User-submitted ratings and reviews rank high both in favorable reactions of customers and ROI for merchants. While Amazon, eBags, and other sites have offered customer reviews for years, merchant adoption has recently soared—both because there's a wealth of evidence that customer reviews lift conversion rate, and because the cost to implement through a third party like Bazaarvoice or PowerReviews has come down so low (it's effectively zero with PowerReviews, which works on an affiliate revenue model).

Freedman points out several merchants that recently launched such features, including The Knot and REI. "Most merchants do start out being nervous about the prospect of negative reviews, but it turns out not to be a problem. A combination of positive and negative reviews is seen as trustworthy by customers. And one person's negative is another person's positive: One customer may say 'the fit is too loose,' but for me, that may be just fine."

Online Chat

Another interactive tool gaining traction with retailers is online text chat between a shopper and a customer service or sales agent. Back in the day, you'll remember, merchants were excited by the notion that online orders would be higher-margin transactions, thanks to their do-it-yourself nature, liberated from costly phone center agents. And that's certainly true—but it's also true that even the best-performing website is unlikely to match the conversion rates of an inbound call center. In my experience, they're different beasts by a factor of ten: picture 5% website sales conversion rates and 50% phone agent conversion rates.

So you're happy to transact high-margin business from self-directed web shoppers. But you'd love to create a higher-touch, higher-conversion connection, with any shoppers who need it—namely anyone who is confused, on the fence, or otherwise ripe for shopping-cart abandonment.

The answer for many merchants is real-time online text chat. With the advent of inexpensive and easily installed chat systems like InstantService and LivePerson, merchants have realized they can offer online shoppers the convenience of human customer service without asking them to pick up the telephone.

"You're either a company that believes in customer service, or you're not," notes Freedman. "If you're a company like Orvis or REI, with a strong commitment to customer service, you're going to have a high close rate with these tools." She noted some firms close 90% of the sales initiated with website-driven online chat.

Click to Call (or CTC) technology, or click-for-a-callback are other angles on the same idea. CTC vendor Estara has released studies claiming a 22% to 25% reduction in site abandonment from pages with click-to-call services—and 143% ROI for the call-to-click investment. But these services have proven much more naturally suited for web enabled phones than to desktops, and they have been slow to catch on. On the advertising side, Google launched, then pulled, CTC advertising with its Google Local search results listings.

But the environment is changing, thanks to VOIP phones. Click-to-call features are part of the Vonage and Skype browser toolbars, which means many of the customers most inclined to click-to-call already have that feature available to them when browsing your site.

Oh, and the low-tech way to bridge this very same gap? Display your 1-800 number prominently on your main navigation!

Social Shopping

With the explosion of interest in social networks, some ecommerce merchants are looking to apply the same dynamic to shopping. At its best, shopping is an inherently social activity. New sites like StyleHive, Kaboodle, wists, and others aim to bring the fun of shopping to an online social network, encouraging shoppers to rate products, share opinions, and compare their tastes with a network of friends.

Mainstream retailers like Wal-Mart are getting into the game too: during the back-to-school season, Wal-Mart partnered with Facebook to launch a "Roommate Style Watch" group, letting a network of college buddies compare notes on their dorm-room shopping plans.

For teens and tweens, Sears created an application using VirtualModel—a 3-D avatar that can be dressed in selected clothing. The tool, called "e-Me," allowed kids to save, print, and share their assembled outfits. The promotion, however, was short-lived and it's unclear, in this case and others, where the real potential of social shopping lies.

Keeping up with the Joneses

It seems clear that on ecommerce sites, both merchants and customers alike take a conservative approach, appreciating some proven Web 2.0 tools, but being cautious about overcomplicating or slowing down the shopping experience.

But a somewhat different picture emerges when we ask shoppers not just about their *most important features*, but of *all the features they now expect* of a site. A 2006 J.C. Williams Group study[28] found that web visitors have come to anticipate a slew of features including many we would put in the Web 2.0 bucket:

- 71% Keyword search
- 64% Product comparison
- 64% Image zoom/rotate
- 60% Catalog quick order
- 60% Customer reviews
- 55% Order history
- 54% Alternate product views
- 54% Loyalty program
- 51% What's New Section
- 51% Recently viewed products
- 45% Related/recommended products
- 45% Customized content
- 41% Live chat
- 39% Audio or video clips
- 39% Wish list
- 39% Best sellers listing
- 35% Gift suggestions
- 31% Discussion boards/blogs

The message here is that today's online shoppers expect websites to offer them interactive shopping tools, rich images, and other media, customer-created reviews, and a variety of different ways to contact the merchant for help. If you're not moving forward on all these fronts, you'll be left behind by your competition.

"It's important to be innovative," concludes Lauren Freedman, but online retailers should be sure they've taken care of their Web 1.0 basics before jumping on the Web 2.0 bandwagon. "If their search doesn't work, I'm not going to be worried about whether they're doing rich media or not."

Search

As if this whole Web 1.0, Web 2.0 thing wasn't arbitrary and confusing enough, the web search guru, Danny Sullivan, muddies it even more by suggesting we've been through two significant phases of search and are now, already, experiencing Search 3.0.

Sullivan founded the successful and influential Search Engine Strategies conference, which now holds several events a year in the United States, Paris, Hamburg, Milan, Tokyo, and elsewhere. He moved on to the editor-in-chief role at SearchEngineLand, and now programs the up-and-coming Search Marketing Expo, or SMX conference series. Danny Sullivan sees the evolution of search this way:

> *Search 1.0* was all about the words on a web page. Results were governed by what Sullivan calls "location, frequency and on-the-page ranking criteria." It worked, but spammy repetition of keywords became a common tactic to climb to the top.
>
> *Search 2.0* was launched by Brinn and Page and their Google algorithm, which added "off-the-page criteria" to the mix. Now the links among websites could be interpreted as signs of popularity and relevance.
>
> So what is *Search 3.0*? Sullivan sees it as Google's "Universal Search." We'll talk more about Universal Search a little later, but in essence it's opening the separate silos Google maintained for different types of data—like videos, news, local listings, stock financials, images, and maps—and intermixing them with the normal text-based web pages that comprise Google's core search index.

Like Google, Yahoo!, MSN, and Ask have all recently pulled down the walls between the various content types in their databases. Some have done so by displaying "related items" or making search suggestions.

That may not sound like a big deal, but it's an important shift in delivering relevant search results. With Universal Search, Google demonstrates that it not only knows the difference between "Hilton Paris" and "Paris

Hilton." It knows when somebody searches for the former, they want a hotel website. When they search the latter, they want lots of celebrity photos and videos.

The major engines are leveraging their historical data on search behavior to deliver more and more relevant results: local results when your query includes a zip code, stock charts when you type a stock symbol, and product comparisons when you search "Blackberry 8800." The future of search is to read your mind.

Predictive Search

Anyone seeking the future of search need look no further than http://www.google.com/mentalplex/, wherein Google revealed its MentalPlex,™ a whirling icon that knows what you want before you even type. The instructions were simple:

- Remove hat and glasses.
- Peer into MentalPlex circle. DO NOT MOVE YOUR HEAD.
- Project mental image of what you want to find.

The MentalPlex was a 2000 April Fool's Day joke. (No one knows how many hapless searchers actually bought it!)

But today it may be closer to reality than we guessed.

Predictive searches, and personalized search results, use stored history to generate suggestions more relevant to each user.

Yahoo! has some robust search prediction tools, called Search Suggest and Search Assist, which build off of the characters typed into the search box to suggest words, phrases, variations, and related searches before you're done typing. Google's toolbar makes similar suggestions governed by popular searches and your own search history.

Increasingly, when any two users perform an identical search, they'll see different results pages. In effect, no two results pages will be alike.

Up to this point, Google's search algorithm, and latterly those of its competitors, has weighed the relevance of particular pages for particular searches by (1) indexing the page's content; (2) gauging the other sites linking to the page; and (3) considering the text used when linking to the page.

That approach yields high-quality results for searches like, say, "Apple Computer," a phrase that has essentially one meaning. But what are the best results for a search for "apple"? It depends. Am I looking for pages about the computer company? Or the Beatles' record company, the musician Fiona Apple, or the humble fruit? How can the search engine possibly know?

Behavioral and demographic data—the kind of information being gathered and acted upon to serve better-targeted advertisements, every moment by all the ad-serving platforms we discussed earlier—are the best clues for improving organic search results. Language preference and content-filtering preference (to avoid seeing pages with sexual content, for instance) are already settings that affect your personal search results. Knowing my gender, where I live, what web pages I have visited, and how I have responded to previous results pages, the search engine can make a much more educated guess about the intent behind my search query.

Your IP address reveals your geographical location. If you're in Chicago searching for "football," you'll get different results than if you perform the same search in London.

If you establish a Google account and log in, Google's personalized search can reorder your search results based on your past searches and clicks, giving more weight to topics that interest you.

If you search for "fly fishing," your future results for a search on "bass" will be weighted more heavily toward fishing than to a guitar, says Google support engineer Maile Ohye. Likewise, if your search history includes searches for golf clubs and handicaps, your search for "golf" will be weighted toward the game and away from the Volkswagen car.

Going forward, just as the paid-search system rewards popular ads with a higher quality score, the organic side could reward the most popular results for a search, and even track click-backs (visitors who use the back button to return to the results page to try another result) as a measure of dissatisfaction.

Should personalized search really take off, no two results pages will be the same. I've heard SEO professionals wryly say it could make their jobs easier: Their client's homepages would likely climb the rankings—at least on their clients' computers!

Vertical Search Engines

It doesn't take Nostradamus to predict that the future of search looks a lot like the past and present of search: Google, Google, and more Google. But a number of search entrepreneurs are saying, "if you can't beat 'em, change the game." Acknowledging that the Big Three have cornered the general search market, they've launched niche search engines devoted to a particular subject area or content type.

Also called vertical search engines or topical search engines, they carve out territory the major engines do poorly. Pixsy and Blinkx index videos, and nothing but videos; Blinkx even uses speech recognition technology to apply text searches to keyword phrases found in videos, audio, and podcasts.

Mamma still maintains its general search-engine index, but it has also created MammaHealth for health, medical, pharmaceutical, and related pages. It built MammaJobs to be "The Mother of all Job Search Engines."

ThisNext and Like.com apply social networking to comparison shopping—a new vertical dubbed "social shopping."

There are verticals devoted to people search, questions-and-answers, legal search engines, product comparison, news, blogs, and images. Because they specialize, they can make a plausible claim that their results are of better quality for certain types of searches.

Having trouble keeping all these niche search tools straight? Check out WhoNu—the vertical search-engine specializing in vertical search-engines!

Local Search

By far the hottest area of vertical search is in local search—the battle to morph the venerable Yellow Pages into a Web 2.0 business model. YellowPages.com, Superpages, MapQuest, and local offerings from Google, Yahoo!, and others are doing a better and better job serving local business results, driving directions and maps, ratings and reviews. We're also witnessing the birth of specialized local search tools, like a MasterCard-sponsored service that helps mobile users find nearby ATM machines. For PDAs and smart phones, local search is the killer app. Everyone needs it, and the payoff to advertisers is clear.

With cell phones driving the future of local search, expect to see tighter integration with GPS—so you won't have to tell the search engine where you are. A little further down the pike will be voice-activated search, so you'll merely need to request "pizza" or "plumber" or "towing service" to generate relevant, local search results.

Social Search

Wikipedia founder Jimmy Wales writes, "Search is part of the fundamental infrastructure of the internet. And it is currently broken. Why? It's broken for the same reason that proprietary software is always broken: lack of freedom, lack of community, lack of accountability, lack of transparency. Wikia Search will start to change all that."

Wales's Wikia Search is built wiki-style, on the principles of openness, collaboration, and community standards. Currently in its alpha version at http://www.alpha.search.wikia.com, Wikia Search acknowledges that the quality of its initial search results are pretty poor—but it's banking on the power of crowdsourcing, hoping that its legion of volunteers will produce a final product as influential and self-correcting as Wikipedia itself.

Mahalo is another self-consciously Web 2.0 search-engine approach, also using wiki development and a healthy dollop of human judgment as its ranking algorithm. Founded by Silicon Valley serial entrepreneur Jason Calacanis, it sounds a lot like the original Yahoo! Directory reenergized around a wiki and social bookmarking. "Google's mission is to index the world's information; our mission is to curate that wonderful index," explains Calacanis. "It is my belief that humans can play a significant role in the development of search results, and we are going to figure out exactly what that role is over the next couple of years"[29]

Speaking of social bookmarking, you could say that sites like Digg, Reddit, Stumbleupon, and del.icio.us are also social search-engines. While they may present their data differently, they basically rank web pages by popularity. While Google pioneered the idea that links were a sign of popularity, the bookmarking sites basically say, "Hey, *popularity* is a sign of popularity."

The Deep Web

In addition to biased data, an ambitious search engine needs to tackle the problem of *hidden* data: the universe of information that's out of reach of traditional web crawlers. Called the "Invisible Web" or the "Deep Web," it consists of data unknown to the search engines because it is called dynamically from databases by uncrawlable websites, or sealed up in video, audio, and Flash files and other content types the text-based crawlers can't fully understand. The deep web dwarfs the entire visible web—it's estimated to be some 550 times bigger.

Add the information that was never digital to begin with, and the visible web has merely scratched the surface.

A number of approaches have attempted to tackle the Deep Web. One with a financial motive is Yahoo! Search Inclusion—a pay-per-click service that lets companies upload their data for inclusion among Yahoo!'s otherwise organic results.

As for bringing offline data online, Google aims to scan and index every book ever published. This is an exhausting project, and not without its setbacks—enterprising visitors to Google Books can occasionally find images of the hands and fingers of scanner operators among the digitized pages.

Smaller do-it-yourself Google initiatives include Google Catalogs, which digitizes mail-order catalogs, and Google Base, which empowers users to upload any sort of structured databases, from baseball cards to recipes, personal ads to products.

The data undiscovered by the web is so massive, we can expect many interesting developments as search players large and small jostle for bigger shares of the pie—and invent better ways of presenting it to searchers.

Universal Search

While vertical search-engines are springing up to segregate specialized data, Google is heading the other direction. With its 2007 introduction of Universal Search, Google began breaking down the walls between content types that previously had lived in their respective silos on specialized search sites: images, videos, news, blogs, maps, and local business listings.

Google Maps, Google News, Google Image Search, etc., all still maintain their own sequestered identities, but they have also now tumbled out onto the billions of Google search results pages that are the site's heart, soul and #1 product. Yahoo! followed suit in much the same way.

"Universal Search strives to be about comprehensiveness and relevance," says Jack Menzel, Universal Search Product Manager at Google.[30] New content types and presentation formats are rolling out constantly, being tested and tweaked: stock quotes, definitions, weather forecasts. Sometimes these new elements are added to the traditional ten-results-on-a-page, sometimes they supplant some of them.

While Yahoo! and Google's intent is to create richer and more relevant results pages, they also present new challenges to businesses wanting to rank well for the keywords germane to their business. For instance, one of the companies I work with, the Vermont chocolatier Lake Champlain Chocolates, now not only has to compete with rival web pages but also music videos like "Chocolate Rain" and comedian Eric Schwartz's parody Hanukkah rap "Chocolate Coins."

In addition to its own different results types, Google now lets users supplement its pages with custom data gleaned from scores of third-party specialists. Called "Subscribed Links," they run the gamut, including weather forecasts, local gas prices, food nutrition info, ski area snow reports, flight arrivals and departures, prescription drug data, recipes, Diggs, even video game cheats. Think of it as widgets, meet RSS feeds, meet search!

From a business perspective, Universal Search mainly ups the ante for your search-engine optimization program. If you want strong organic search results for your company's name, its market, its products, and other key phrases, you now need to concern yourself not just with your web pages, but also with a slew of other indexed data. Companies should be investing in all the content that Google and the other search engines are spidering and indexing. Most companies should have not only a website, but also a blog and presences in social media. They should create local business listings if they don't already exist, issue regular online press releases, and get creative about putting good, relevant, video content online.

And then are you done? Unfortunately, no. This first iteration of Universal Search will no doubt be joined by anything else Google and its rivals can make sense of. GoogleBase and Google Product Search are terrific sourcing grounds for all sorts of delimited data that could make good additions to the Google SERPs (that's "search-engine results page"). The goal will be to create more relevant results for the user—but the impact for web businesses will be a constant and everchanging challenge to maintain high visibility in their market, every time the search-engines expand their reach into new media types.

5 ▪ ▪ ▪

Successful Online Business Models for Web 2.0 and Beyond

With over a decade's worth of hindsight, we now have some perspective on business models that work online—and some that crash and burn. The churning survival-of-the-fittest process, which continues to operate in the financial markets and ecommerce at large, has produced stupendous winners and stunning failures.

Those frothy early dotcom business plans assumed that digital commerce would rewrite the rules, allowing companies to launch with virtually no fixed expenses and scale massively thereafter.

But Pets.com learned the hard way that massive media buys featuring a sock-puppet mascot didn't change the realities of the pet supplies business: Physical goods offer just so much gross margin, and to sell them requires operational investments from warehouses to trucking and phone centers; eToys was pretty much the same story. Other high-profile Web 1.0 flops like the delivery services Webvan and Kozmo demonstrated that when your "online" business requires you to pay for trucks, gas, and couriers, you need more than a few pints of ice cream worth of revenue to keep it afloat.

Pure-play digital companies like eBay have delivered better on rule-changing dotcom business models, capturing a share of the transactions made on its network, but staying out of the costly business of storing, photographing, and shipping products. Amazon leveraged the web to achieve unparalleled market share ("Earth's Biggest Selection" as Amazon puts it), but even with its strong commitment to enabling a virtual marketplace of third-party sellers, Amazon's profit margins are decidedly tied to the earth.

Google, on the other hand, pays plenty for its server farms, campuses, and army of top-flight engineers and executives, yet still produces financial results scarcely heard of before the internet. By the fourth quarter of 2007 (a quarter in which investors punished it for disappointing them), Google yielded over 36% net profit on sales of about $3.4 billion.[1]

In fact, Google is in large measure responsible for cementing a business model that works for countless smaller online players. Its ubiquitous online ads—and the revenue share that smaller sites get for displaying them—have succeeded in that elusive goal of the Web 1.0 era: "monetizing the eyeballs."

When I describe the basic ecommerce business models below, my focus is on businesses that can depend largely or totally on online revenues. There are many successful publishers, B2B (business to business) service companies, brand marketers, and others, whose websites play an enormous and successful role in getting the word out, generating sales leads, or establishing positive brand identity. Their internet strategies may be fascinating and their accomplishments real, but I won't include them in our discussion of online business models.

The major established models are:

- Online Retail
- Advertising-Supported
- Subscription Model
- Download Fees
- Affiliate Marketing
- Software-as-a-Service
- Brokerage or Intermediary

As we'll see, many businesses have hybrid business models combining a number of these. Hybrid business models are fairly easy to pursue online, more so than in the bricks-and-mortar world; it's feasible to present a fairly straightforward face to the web visitor, while stitching together a number of different online revenue models and operational systems behind the scenes. But as we'll discuss later in the chapter, just because it's possible to chase many models at once doesn't mean it's a good idea!

▒ Online Retail

Call it "eTail," "Retail eCommerce," or just "eCommerce," the business of selling physical goods online has grown at a double-digit clip for over a decade, and now stands at over $130 billion a year in the United States. According to the Commerce Department, there's still plenty of room to grow, as internet retailing still represents less than 4% of the total retail industry.[2]

The web has played havoc with some bricks-and-mortar retailers, especially in broad-and-shallow markets like books, music, and movies, where it's impossible for any local retailer to accurately anticipate and satisfy demand. No wonder those segments have migrated so dramatically to the 800-lb gorillas: Amazon, iTunes, and Netflix.

On balance, though, the rise of ecommerce has been very kind to small local firms, direct-mail catalogers, and niche businesses. Prior to the commercial web, these companies had to content themselves with their local markets, or pay costly print and postage bills to mail catalogs to the outside world. Thanks to free search traffic, small specialty companies and mom-and-pops could now be discovered by customers far and wide, and it was "found money." The advent of paid search allowed such companies to invest in direct-response advertising with none of the obstacles of traditional media: There was no minimum ad buy, no fixed costs, it was easy to track spending to actual results in real time, and you could ramp your advertising up or shut it off entirely in response to performance.

These dynamics explain why the web, as viewed through the typical search results page, is still a much more democratic place, much more hospitable to small merchants, than is a typical mall or high-rent retail district, the glossy pages of national magazines, or mainstream broadcast media. One reason is inventory: There's a physical limit on desirable retail locations; there are only a hundred or so ad pages in each issue of Oprah's magazine, only one Super Bowl. But the inventory of search results, and impressions on informational and entertainment websites, is essentially limitless. What's more, the particular niche interest revealed by a searcher's query—what John Battelle calls the "database of intentions"—can make it profitable for online merchants to go after even the smallest of niches.

If you don't believe me, go to your favorite search engine and search for anything carried by several big, national retailers: shoes, purses, potato chips, men's shirts, basketballs, cordless drills. You'll see a lot more Davids than Goliaths among the results. Even the paid ads are populated with a disproportionate share of small, entrepreneurial players and ecommerce pure-plays.

That said, if there's one myth the dotcom bust disproved, it's "if you build it, they will come." They *won't* come, not unless you start with remarkable products, couple them with customer service and a company philosophy that people want to talk about, and support it with a realistic marketing and PR budget.

Nielsen NetRatings regularly releases lists of the online stores with the highest sales conversion rates, the percentage of all visitors who completed a purchase.[3] Its top-ten list for holiday season 2007 looked like this:

- The Popcorn Factory, 29.5%
- L.L. Bean, 23.6%
- Abe Books, 20.6%
- Amazon.com, 17.6%
- Hollister Company, 17.6%
- Lands' End, 17.2%
- Coldwater Creek, 17.1%
- QVC, 17.1%
- Cabela's, 16.8%
- Gymboree, 16.0%

Conversion rates don't necessarily say anything about a store's profitability, but they do tell us that visitors to these sites were strongly motivated to purchase. Traditionally, the best converting sites are dominated by big catalog companies like Bean, Land's End, Coldwater Creek, and Cabela's—firms that invest heavily in print catalogs to drive consumers to their sites, ready to buy. So should small niche marketers despair if their conversion rates are mired in the low single digits? Not necessarily, if they're attracting those less targeted customers for little or no money, through tactics like organic search-engine optimization, word-of-mouth, online community outreach, PR, or guerilla marketing.

In recent years, online retailers have been trying to make sense of *multichannel marketing*—how best to attribute costs and sales when they are spread across several different channels, like catalogs, online advertising, or physical retail stores, each of which plays some role in driving sales. Conventional marketing thinking tells us all these multiple touch-points should work together to turn prospects into buyers: Ideally, the whole is more than the sum of the parts.

But, in reality, the multichannel Web 2.0 world is causing online marketers to reevaluate that thinking. Do all these marketing messages really pull their weight in creating the sale—or do some deserve more aggressive investment at the expense of others? Could some channels be eliminated altogether without damage to the bottom line? Kevin Hillstrom, a marketing analyst and veteran of Eddie Bauer, Lands End, and Nordstrom, told participants at a 2007 conference about strategies for quantifying the contributions of different channels.[4] For instance, a marketer with a big enough catalog or email list, like Nordstrom, can hold back segments of those lists, comparing, say, a segment of customers receiving no emails with a segment receiving no print catalogs, versus the control group of customers receiving the entire regimen.

Hillstrom, now the principal of a Seattle-based consultancy called Marketing Forensics, further recommends that businesses analyze their overall customer repurchase behavior, and migration patterns across brands, product groups, or marketing channels. The goal is to quantify the degree to which they're operating in customer-acquisition mode versus customer-retention mode, and also to identify customer migrations across different marketing channels. For instance, your primary customer-acquisition method may be broadcast radio, while most repurchases are driven by your email program. The company as a whole is trending toward customer-retention mode, but each channel has its own profile for customer retention and migration. As a business leader, you need to know the characteristics and trends of each, and invest proportionally in each to drive the most profitable marketing mix for top-line growth and repeat business.

How has Web 2.0 changed the overall business model for retailing? The most profound changes have to do with reach beyond local markets and local tastes, and the ability to offer enormously broad inventories—the phenomenon coined and expertly described by Chris Anderson in his book, *The Long Tail*. Today there is no disincentive to offer the entire universe of products of potential interest to your customers. Perhaps you won't physically stock the smallest sellers, but thanks to drop-shipping, just-in-time inventory, and affiliate relationships, there's no effective limit on the merchandise an online retailer can carry. That includes not only prefab products but on-demand, custom ones as well: coffee mugs, tee-shirts, campaign buttons, bumper stickers, imprinted water bottles, and self-published books from places like Café Press, Motivators.com, CustomInk, and Lulu.

Anderson points out that the web has enabled so many people to effortlessly search for and find so many items that the "hits" are now vastly outnumbered by the "misses"—the area under the long tail is far greater than that under the steep head of bestsellers.

The lower overhead of online retailers, when compared to brick-and-mortar firms, amounts to generally healthier profit margins. Piper Jaffray's senior internet analyst, Safa Rashtchy, told the 2006 Shop.org Annual Summit that publicly held ecommerce retailers averaged about 14% margins, double that of traditional retailers.[5] However, these profits are increasingly squeezed by rising customer acquisition and shipping costs.

Going forward, the Web 2.0 challenge of the typical ecommerce retailer will be to further take advantage of the long tail, and to use customer segmentation to reach out to existing customers to better market to those countless specialized niches. And the typical ecommerce retail site is still very ripe for Web 2.0 improvements: They can be far more dynamic, more entertaining, and more social experiences.

"I strongly believe we will see a sense of community, imagination, and entertainment infiltrate our ecommerce websites," ventures Kevin Hillstrom. "While ecommerce functionality will still be important, it is clear that something has been missing. We've built ecommerce websites that lack warmth, and lack interaction."

▥ Advertising-Driven

Advertising revenues are looking like an irresistible force lately, demonstrating an awesome ability to "monetize" all sorts of informational and multimedia content, and social-networking activity. Almost any popular online pursuit, from gaming to dating to texting on your phone, is increasingly perceived as a platform for ad revenues.

What's largely driving this trend is the revenue-share that the major search engines bestow on other websites that display their ads. The ad platforms call these myriad other websites their "content network." Another way to look at it is that Google and the other players are syndicating their ads out onto third-party websites, in exchange for a cut of the money.

Google, Yahoo!, and MSN have had a good deal of success in taking ads originally intended for their search results pages, and syndicating them across "content pages"—news sites, blogs, forums, etc. The ad platforms have also enabled display advertising for this network of content sites, and other players are attracting advertisers with behavioral targeting and other sophisticated strategies. Advertisers are rushing in, looking for new potential customers. That trend has been a boon for publishers small and large, creating a business model for many sites that long found revenue elusive.

Still, the online advertising ecosystem is not completely healthy. Despite pains that these ad platforms have taken to improve quality, in my experience and those of many marketers I talk to, the content networks just don't deliver direct-response results. The engines offer separate bidding control over clicks from the content network, but the lure of revenue-share money has brought a lot of low-quality sites out of the woodwork. Dubbed "MFA," or "Made for AdSense," these sites clutter the search results and mar the experience of many a web user. You find them well-ranked among the organic search results for something you're seeking, but when you click through, you see an ugly and unhelpful page serving up nothing but columns of paid text links. They bear no signs of purposeful human design and editing. In fact, many of them are automatically generated by harvesting and randomly repurposing the content of "real" pages out on the internet—blog posts, press releases, and the like.

Alan Rimm-Kaufman, former Crutchfield VP of Marketing and a longtime veteran of online advertising, leads the Rimm-Kaufman Group, a direct marketing services and consulting firm founded in 2003 in Charlottesville, VA. He identified thousands of AdSense-supported pages generated automatically, in the space of just 48 hours, through spidering and screen-scraping of a newly created page on his site. "Trash pages set up by spiders run by Bad Guys to rip off online advertisers," Rimm-Kaufman calls them. "Because of the business model Google established, AdSense spam flourishes. Google's battle to keep Bad Guys out of content increases in difficulty every day."[6]

A sustainable revenue model for content-providing websites is a good thing—it could be the motor that drives great mobile applications, robust social networks, and more. But it won't live up to that promise until it provides value to the advertisers. While there's ample evidence of trouble, Rimm-Kaufman sees light at the end of the tunnel. "Historically our agency has found the content networks weak, but we're now seeing signs of some improvement from Google content clicks. We take that as evidence that Google's getting better at keeping trash sites out the content network."

▨ Subscription Model

Web users have a venerable tradition of refusing to subscribe to content—even the best content. The publishing businesses that pioneered the subscription model offline have oft been foiled trying to make a go of the same model online.

In 1984, about a decade before the dawn of the commercial web, author and *Whole Earth Catalog* founder Stewart Brand addressed the first Hackers Convention in Marin, CA, and coined the expression "information wants to be free."[7]

"On the one hand information wants to be expensive," he remarked, "because it's so valuable. The right information in the right place just changes your life. On the other hand, information wants to be free, because the cost of getting it out is getting lower and lower all the time. So you have these two fighting against each other."

Indeed, information and entertainment have shown a penchant for being free online. Back in the pre-bubble days, Slate abandoned its subscription model in less than a year. *The LA Times* threw in the towel on its paid subscription model, as did *The New York Times*, *The Economist*, and *The Financial Times*. AOL finally bagged its ISP subscription model. CNN abandoned trying to sell paid subs to its "Pipeline" online video service.

"CNN.com is finally realizing that nobody wants to pay for video online," wrote Erick Schonfeld in Business 2.0's blog.[8] "It is much easier to get advertisers to pay $20 to $40 per thousand viewers for a video ad than it is to get consumers to fork over an extra $25 a year for something similar to what they can already get on basic cable. The hunger among advertisers for video inventory that they can put their brands behind (as opposed to YouTube videos) is so strong right now, that it makes no sense for any media company to hide their videos behind a subscription wall."

Not that subscription revenues are anything to sneeze at—in just a few years *The New York Times*' TimesSelect service generated some $20 million in revenue.[9] It's just that it's dwarfed by the advertising revenue potential of tearing down the walls and exposing content to multitudes of searchers and other visitors.

Nevertheless, a number of segments have proven able to charge subscriptions. The twin vices of pornography and online gambling no doubt rake in the most chips. Adult-entertainment industry analyst AVN reckoned subscription and product sales at pornography sites tallied $2.8 billion in 2006.[10]

While many online dating sites are free to users, a select few—Match.com, eHarmony, and Yahoo! Personals, for instance—are able to charge monthly membership fees to at least some of their audience.

Financial and market research sites have effectively managed paid-subscription or pay-per-access models, usually exposing just a brief abstract of a topic or report to the search-engine spiders, and charging for full access. Examples include eMarketer, Forrester, Jupiter, and Hoovers. Some subscription models go where the money is, as with employment site Monster.com, where job seekers generally participate for free, but companies and headhunters have to pay to play.

While big media companies have yet to crack a mainstream subscription model that works, niche publishers have fared better, simply because their information is less widely available and generally more relevant and vital to their core audience. One example is PublishersMarketplace.com, where publishing insiders can access news of the latest publishing deals: who, what, and—critically—how much. Another niche subscription-driven

site is for pundits, lobbyists, wonks, and political junkies: PollingRe-
port.com, serving up-to-the-moment polling data on state, local, and nationwide election campaigns, political approval ratings, and more. Value
of the data is one key to success, and the other is price: Even for niche
sites, you're likely to see modest subscription fees like $9 or $19 a month.

Netflix, which at the time of writing this book has over 7 million paid
subscribers and $1.2 billion a year in revenue, gets the lion's share of
its income from subscription fees. The company also collects advertising
revenue, and is venturing into paid downloads as well.

Though it may be a stretch to think of it as a subscription business
model, online education has been a bright spot for Web 2.0. Online college programs have overcome initial skepticism, and some low-quality
programs, to evolve into some really innovative programs. In the fall of
2006 almost 3.5 million students—nearly 20% of all U.S. higher education students—were taking at least one online course, according to data
collected by The Sloan Consortium.[11]

Online education has become a mainstream response to the needs especially of working adults seeking postgraduate degrees and professional
training. From Babson to Harvard Extension School, Cornell to many public universities, scores of traditional colleges now offer online courses,
whether they be executive MBAs or continuing education. The University
of Phoenix, which pretty much pioneered the online degree, calls itself the
largest private university in North America. Western Governors University
(WGU) is taking a different approach—a nonprofit initiative founded and
supported by governors of nineteen states, it offers accredited online degree programs in business, information technology, education, and health
care. Its national advisory board includes representatives from some of
the companies most prominent in calling for a better-trained American
workforce, among them Google, Microsoft, Hewlett Packard, Dell, Oracle,
and Sun.

"Google has pioneered the idea of access to information," said Google
CEO Eric Schmidt. "The reason Google thinks WGU is such a good idea is
because WGU has pioneered the concept of competency-based education
whenever you want it."

▓ Download Fees

The paid, legal download model for music was dramatically proven by Apple's iTunes, which launched in 2003 and crossed the 3-billion download
mark in the middle of 2007. While growth has slowed, the point has been
made: If the price is right, customers will choose legal alternatives over

pirate copies. But media companies everywhere still face a challenge of providing pay-for-download content at a price customers will accept.

Apple, Amazon, Microsoft, and Wal-Mart have begun offering consumers the ability to download television programs and movies to own or rent. Netflix and Blockbuster offer downloads not on a fee-for-download basis but as part of a monthly subscription.

The download-to-own (DTO) market has shown more appetite for television episodes, at $1.99 a pop from iTunes and others, than it has for DTO or download-to-rent (DTR) feature films. Google Video folded up its paid video download service in 2007—ironically stymied by its own free, all-you-can-eat video acquisition, YouTube.

Forrester estimated that paid video downloads generated $279 million in revenue in 2007, up from $98 million the previous year. But Forrester predicts a decline in the pay-per-download model, seeing instead an increasing role for advertising in driving the online video market.[12]

"The paid video download market in its current evolutionary state will soon become extinct, despite the fast growth and the millions being spent today," writes Forrester analyst James McQuivey. "Television and cable networks will shift the bulk of paid downloading to ad-supported streams where they have control of ads and effective audience measurement. The movie studios, whose content only makes up a fraction of today's paid downloads, will put their weight behind subscription models that imitate premium cable channel services."

▓ Affiliate Marketing

Until the syndication of paid search ads, affiliate marketing was the only meaningful revenue opportunity for site owners not offering their own products for sale. A notoriously fragmented industry full of many small players, industry size estimates are tough to come by. Even in 2006, MarketingSherpa researchers estimated that worldwide, affiliate marketers raked in a whopping $6.5 billion in commissions and bounties.[13] The monthly magazine of the industry, *Revenue*, often profiles ordinary Joes (and Janes) making comfortable livings or even small fortunes in their bare feet in the comfort of their dens. But that now-stereotypical image of the successful affiliate is really just part of the story. Affiliate-driven businesses now include big, well-established companies like PriceGrabber, NextTag, FabulousSavings.com, MyPoints, and UPromise.

Affiliate compensation can be a sales revenue share, or a bounty for an action such as lead generation, new membership, catalog request, or newsletter sign up. In the technology and B2B spaces, affiliation can take the form of re-seller agreements, implementation partnerships, and other revenue-sharing arrangements.

Software-as-a-Service

Software-as-a-Service (SaaS) is an enormous segment of online business—an estimated $9 billion, as discussed in Chapter 3. The range of successful SaaS companies is stunning, and it ranges from modest little $19 a month applications to full-fledged enterprise software delivered on demand across the net. Practically, an on-demand software provider signs up its customers and establishes an account with browser-based username and password access. The billing model may be a monthly fee charged to a credit card, a set contract, or a usage-based charge.

As large as the SaaS industry already is, we're really just seeing the dawn of it now. Without exaggeration, it's possible to foresee a time when most software applications will be delivered on demand this way. The two approaches are either to access the web to download and install new applications or updates onto your computer, or—increasingly common—to access applications hosted remotely, on the provider's web servers.

The familiar online Windows Update process is essentially software as a service—albeit a free one. Even when software is packaged and delivered on disk, like TurboTax, it will increasingly look across the internet for updates, security patches, up-to-the-moment data sources, and to integrate via web services with third-parties (in the Turbo Tax example, these might be brokerage firms and mutual fund companies, major employers, etc.).

But the real growth in SaaS will come from on-demand web applications. These include enterprise class software like SalesForce, ecommerce platforms, email campaign management platforms—even a blog-publishing account is essentially software as a service. Online videoconferencing and collaboration tools capture just one vibrant segment of the whole: WebEx, HP Halo, Cisco Telepresence, Lotus Sametime, Adobe, Connect, are all competing in this space.

On-demand software is a business model truly coming of age in the Web 2.0 era, because it benefits from increased bandwidth, cheap storage, and robust computing power. There are still obstacles, to be sure—you don't want mission-critical applications to be compromised by lapses in your internet access, for instance, nor should you commit all your customer and financial data to outside servers. But SaaS works for customers because there's already a demonstrated willingness to pay for applications like these—it merely shifts the delivery platform from the customer's computers onto the vendors. And by moving applications into the cloud, SaaS also delivers many compelling advantages over traditional software: ongoing updates, real-time integration with third-party services and data, and a pay-as-you-go pricing model.

░ Brokerage or Intermediary

Remember when the rise of the commercial web was hailed as the death-knell of the middleman? How it was going to eliminate all those layers between buyer and seller, and the financial slice of the pie each was taking, ushering in a brave new age of frictionless commerce? I've got news for you: it didn't happen.

Sure, "disintermediation" exacted a heavy toll on middlemen in some markets: travel agents and stockbrokers, for instance, suffered huge migration of individual customers to online travel sites and do-it-yourself discount brokerages. The clear message was that, at least for the little guy, these markets were inefficient, and brokers weren't providing sufficient value. Many consumers felt they could do a better job researching and transacting vacations and stock trades online, and save money in the process.

Of course, in the same process, consumers and sellers were anointing new middlemen, rewarding them with a cut of the business in exchange for the service of information gathering, sorting, and transaction processing. These businesses are of the *brokerage* or *intermediary* business model.

Brokerage-model websites include travel sites like Travelocity, Expedia, and Priceline, stock brokerages like eTrade, car brokerages like Cars.com, and auction platform eBay. Transaction-processors PayPal, Amazon Flexible Payments, and Google Checkout are also brokerage-model businesses. Monster.com and other employment sites run on a brokerage model, extracting fees from employers and recruiters. Specialized brokers include BidNet (for government contracts), ScriptLance (for IT offshoring), Lending Tree (for mortgages), and others.

Brokerage-style online businesses get their fees from the buyer, seller, or both. Oh, about that disintermediation? These new middlemen aren't generally perceived as adding a lot of fat to the transaction, perhaps because they're often free to consumers, and supported by vendors wanting access to the marketplace.

░ Hybrid Online Business Models

Hybrids of the above models are easy to find. Today, businesses can move into a new model as easy as pressing Ctrl-V.

LinkedIn generates roughly equal revenue from three sources: premium subscriptions, advertising sales, and job listings. Most of the subscription-based sites mentioned above also generate advertising revenue. Content sites often supplement advertising revenues with product sales—you can buy tee shirts on BoingBoing and cookbooks on Eating Well. Many commerce sites will direct-ship you the items it stocks, and offer links to other companies with which it has affiliate relationships. Amazon is a great example of a hybrid model. While Amazon's first goal may be to sell you a product in its warehouses, it also gives prime real estate to third-party new and used goods dealers. Whether you want to buy from Amazon or one of its partners is up to you. Don't find what you're looking for when you search? No problem: Amazon will serve up paid ads taking you off the site.

The important thing when embracing one of these bold new Web 2.0 hybrid business models is to do your math. Doubtless Amazon has done the math, and knows how many dollars each visitor is worth, whether she buys a product directly from Amazon, or from one of Amazon's merchant partners and generates a revenue-share, or clicks off the site for a few pennies. The trick is to encourage the behaviors best for your bottom line, and not cannibalize your own sales by granting too much prominence to affiliates and advertisers.

6 ▪ ▪ ▪

Ten Things You Should Do to Make Your Business More "Web 2.0"

These ten ideas are meant to be practical, relatively easy steps that could benefit almost every website, whatever its mission (including nonprofit missions). Some ideas are more relevant to organizations that sell products or services, generate advertising revenue, or generate business leads. But whatever your model is, if you want to embrace some of the cultural and technical trends of Web 2.0, these are great places to start.

eCommerce merchants are in a touchy position when it comes to making Web 2.0 innovations, because they must weigh any hoped-for gain against both the cost of implementation and the potential cost of confusing or distracting visitors from the task of finding and buying products. Probably that's why the Web 2.0 features that are enjoying the fastest uptake on ecommerce sites are ones with clear connections to improving the purchase conversion rate:

- Enhanced product images
- Product reviews and ratings
- Personalization
- Live customer-service chat

Some Web 2.0 innovations seem promising, but aren't for everyone—for instance, they may demand too much time from a typically brief user session. For social-media features to be successful, you must operate in a market that stirs people's passions enough to get them interacting with their online social circle. For mobile applications to benefit you, your offerings must be a natural fit for on-the-go customers.

Another challenge is to quantify the lift, or improvement, of a new Web 2.0 feature. Realtime A/B tests are the preferred method, because when two versions of your site are delivered simultaneously to two randomly selected segments of your customers, the test quantifies the benefit of a new feature—without introducing any other timing-related variables (like seasonality, marketing mix, product availability) that would muddy the waters. Multivariate tests, which serve up more than one variation, are also valuable because they identify the best combination of several options.

Before testing, you have to identify what "best" outcomes mean to you. If you're selling products, you'll look for increased sales conversion rates, or average order value (or both!). If your site is ad-supported, your goal may be to increase visits, page-views, and visit duration. Social-media features might be weighed in terms of repeat visits, and traffic coming from referrals to friends. And you'll also want to track the numbers most directly associated with your Web 2.0 initiatives: How many people are posting and reading product reviews? How many are establishing profiles, what is the average number of friend links, how many forum postings, RSS subscriptions, visits to your .mobi site, signups for your mobile text-messaging program, links into your site from the blogosphere? To spot trends, you should track some metrics not just in their raw numbers, but also as a portion of the total. For example, what portion of all customers are registered users? What percentage of business leads is coming from the mobile site?

Idea 1. Participate in Your Relevant Online Community

"As people get more used to social networking they want more flexibility," said Ning cofounder, Marc Andreessen, from the podium at the exclusive Web 2.0 Summit in San Francisco.[1] "It's a really important step to un-lock the creativity people have." And so it is: Putting tools for expression and personal connection into the hands of your customers is a win-win. It energizes them, deepens their connection with your brand and their favorite aspects of the market you serve; it lets them comfortably bring others into the network and authentically vouch for the quality of their favorite items and services. And you, as the host of the network, bolster your connection to the topic and your audience—to better know them, interact with them, and learn from them.

Towering above the forest are popular, influential, and (if they so choose) profitable blogs. Top sites like TechCrunch, Engadget, BoingBoing, and the Huffington Post typically rank among the top 1,000 most-visited sites on the web.

But chances are, you do business in a niche or subcategory, and here is where blogs really shine. Niche blogs draw smaller but passionate and community-spirited audiences. No doubt there are many blogs serving your industry, and many others written by and devoted to your customers, whether they are knitters, or Celtic music lovers, or amateur astronomers.

So the answer to how you should be participating in the blogosphere:

1. Read, comment on, and link to good blogs in your industry.
2. Read the blogs in your target market; get to know the leading bloggers and incorporate them respectfully in your media, advertising, and public relations planning.
3. Create your own company blog to communicate in a more timely, personal, or interactive way than is possible on your principal website.

Following is a little more detail on these blog strategies.

Participate in Industry Blogs

We all need a healthy network of business contacts, and today the life and development of a network takes place, in good measure, online. Being an active, respectful, generous participant in the blogging and networking of others is a Web 2.0 virtue.

Perhaps you have it in you to create your own blog, and link to the best posts of others. If you can't make that commitment, use your Facebook, LinkedIn, Technorati, and other profile pages to point others in the direction of your favorite bloggers. Being connected online is an important part of your reputation and visibility, personally and for your company and its offerings. Don't do it for visibility's sake—do it because it's right. Be selective about whose blogs you read and judicious in how you respond, whom you add to your network, and what content you Digg and pass around. Contrary to popular belief, Web 2.0 networking and communication is about quality, not quantity.

Participate in Blogs in Your Target Markets

This is an exciting part of your Web 2.0 strategy, and one not without its pitfalls. Identify active bloggers and opinion-makers in the target markets you serve. Read their blogs, comment, and link to their relevant posts. For the best and most relevant sites, introduce yourself and learn what opportunities exist for more outreach. Perhaps the blogger welcomes material, and would respond to your press releases, a sneak peek at new products, or would interview one of your people. Maybe she accepts advertising or wants to join your affiliate program. Maybe she would do a product review if you sent her samples, or offer to conduct a reader survey on your behalf. The point is, explore what you can do for one another.

Lake Champlain Chocolates, which makes all-natural, small-batch chocolates, is a good example of a firm that cares passionately about what it does, and connects with its customers on a direct and personal level, as fellow appreciators. When it comes to news releases, product samples, and access to the company, Lake Champlain Chocolates treats bloggers just like other representatives of the media—whether its products are being taste-tested by *Good Housekeeping*, or celebrated on blogs like CandyAddict.com or CandyFreak.com.

For brand marketers and direct marketers alike, this is counterintuitive. Even the biggest bloggers are *small guys* compared to the reach of the typical media buy or PR score. Some may be unprofessional, weird, or a little obsessive. But use your judgment and ideally you'll reach out to a smart, motivated, opinionated, well-connected vanguard—the hubs of their own Web 2.0 networks. If your products deserve it, they will get your stuff noticed, you'll attract links to your site, your search-engine rank will benefit, and you'll have connected with the right people. They are people whose opinions are disproportionately influential, within their niche, and can set a small but viral popularity in motion.

Create Your Company Blog

What could your company, group, or organization have to say—and on a nearly daily basis, no less? If you operate in a rather dry industry, it seems a stretch. And even for a colorful company in a dynamic industry, it's a tough challenge to decide who will be the author and what the brand voice of the thing will be. I'll simplify matters by suggesting the reason to have a blog is to have a daily, informal, newsy, and personal connection with your customers and (maybe) the media. Your main website can't do that— it is busy being a beautifully merchandised online store, or whatever. But the need remains for regular communication to and interaction with your core audience. Again, these are your best customers, and the most influential members of your "community."

Think of the blog not as a marketing vehicle but as a place to (1) communicate timely information about the market you serve, your company, and its stuff, and (2) further establish your brand voice, be it cool and ironic, caring and serious, etc.

A couple of examples of people doing this well:

- The nursing blog at Motherwear, a leading maternity clothing line, is a warm and helpful source of breastfeeding information and advocacy. It doesn't roll out the sales pitches—it demonstrates that it knows and supports the new and expectant moms that are its customers. Motherwear president Tom Kothman saw both tangible and intangible benefits from the blog: 25% of all new visitors came to Motherwear via its blog—and blog visitors placed orders 15% higher than those from other sources. "A blog gives you credibility and supports the brand," he says.[2]
- The Backcountry.com blog strikes the right note of irreverent humor, gear lust, and outdoor sports credibility for its audience.
- Its search pages are devoid of Google content, so if Google wants to talk to its community, blogs and forums are its real estate of choice. The website http://www.Googleblog.Blogspot.com and the dedicated blogs for Gadgets API, OpenSocial APIs, and Android Developers are good examples of both brand voice and functional communication.

Perhaps more relevant to those of us who do direct-marketing within a particular niche or to a particular demographic, there is a thriving and fascinating blogosphere dedicated to everything under the sun, no matter how obscure or cutting edge. Want to sell organic baby clothes, get attention for a book about autism, or introduce an online network for beekeepers? There are blogs and an active online community of experts and enthusiasts out there right now, posting about your topic.

The power of these specialized online niches is really remarkable. You might be tempted to write off a humble blog on, say, knitting, or Persian cats, or kosher food. But if you are responsible for getting word out about your products or services, and you can sensitively and authentically reach out to relevant opinion-makers online, you can make a positive impression on just the sort of influential voices who are your best customers *and* the most effective evangelizers of your stuff to others. A survey by the eTail Group[3] found 75% of web users rank *personal recommendations and ratings* as the single most influential factor inspiring them to make a purchase.

It's not about you, the marketer, telling customers to buy your stuff. It's about consumers telling each other about your stuff.

Another important outreach to make in the Web 2.0 world is into the social networks. Your business needs a well-designed and maintained MySpace page, a Facebook profile, and a lens on Squidoo. You and your colleagues should have professional profiles on LinkedIn or the other business-oriented networks. Depending on your market, you may want to participate in photo- and video-sharing on YouTube, Flickr, and elsewhere. There are probably great niche networks in your field.

But why? What's the purpose, and who are you connecting with?

If you're in B2B, the leap from traditional networking to Web 2.0 networking isn't hard to grasp: present yourself as a source of good, trustworthy information; connect with industry colleagues; ask and answer questions; meet business prospects.

If you're in B2C, and more familiar with mass-media communication with enough people to really move the revenue needle, well, you have to reset your expectations. Web 2.0 social media isn't about sales—quite the opposite. View it as a public commons where motivated, highly connected members of your community gather. Corporate communications types like to call them "stakeholders." Sure, many of them will be customers and prospects, but that's beside the point. Don't come off as opportunistic and simply out for a buck. The social website isn't where people go to buy from you—it's where they go to connect with others, have fun, ask for information, and post their opinions: rants, raves, passions, and frustrations. And among them (wearing perfect camouflage) will be especially important stakeholders: journalists, bloggers, activists, angel investors, and nut jobs. When you interact with them, exemplify the brand values you and your company hold dear. Exude high quality, honesty, fairness, attentiveness, creativity, and a sense of humor!

The jury is still our about how meaningful it is when people "friend" your brand on a social network website. My sense is it all depends on how much of a relationship truly exists. If you're a lifestyle brand, or a niche company, they may be giving you a serious nod, spending some of their hard-won personal credibility to approve of who you are and what you do. In an age of advertising overload, personal recommendations are the real gold standard of Web 2.0—they are the single most important factor that shoppers say influences them.

Examples abound of savvy companies using the social media with cleverness and cultural fit. The snowboard clothing company eeSa, founded by a former Burton brand manager, Stephen Cleary, is a great example: The company's website, its profiles on the social networks, and all its communications, from catalogs to emails and online postings, speak with one voice: the voice of hard-core snowboarders talking with their peers. They're rebels with a sense of humor, obsessed with riding and enjoying the lodge afterwards. They're hooked into relevant online groups, pitching on-mountain events and promotions, sharing shredding videos. With *Snowboard* magazine they launched a "DJ division" and distributed free MP3 mixes to their email list—to promote DJs and to work with the natural connection between music and riding. They reach out to their community online and off, driving an old RV 8,000 miles to ski areas in 13 days (and later selling it on eBay via emails to its community). For this company, friend connections on the social media are real friendships. The company knows its community because it lives, breathes, and rides in it. An earlier era might have called it guerilla marketing, but it's more like antimarketing—more like bona fide community.

Northampton, Massachusetts-based Yarn.com has reached out to its community of knitters and weavers through a thoughtful and colorful blog written by co-owner Kathy Elkins. The Yarn.com website also offers knitting and weaving classes and a Q & A service. Its weekly "Ready, Set, Knit!" radio talk show is available via on-demand audio stream, and podcasts via RSS feed.

If you're interested in exposing a brand, product, service, organization, or leader to the social networks, my advice is to participate in each community first before you target advertising at its members. Join and get to know the social networks and their unique cultures. Create good profiles for your organization or its offerings, complete with images, and contact info for a real person committed to responding personally to any messages and inquiries. Write in informal, straightforward language that captures your personal voice, rather than mushy corporate-speak.

But tread lightly. Treat the social networks as an opportunity for personal interaction, and keep the ads where they belong.

"Let's remember that social networks are about people, not about companies," Seth Godin pointed out to me. "Nobody wants to 'friend' Ford Motor Company. As a result, companies, which are notoriously self-centered, have no place at all in a traditional social network. I'm not there to click on the ads, buddy."

"At the same time," Godin goes on, "Google has made it easy for marketers to place anticipated, personal and relevant ads in front of people who are looking for them. So, I guess the answer is:

- Make stuff that people will choose to talk about;
- Respect people's need for privacy and, yes, quiet;
- Make sure your ads show up in the right place at the right moment."[4]

Idea 2. Launch Customer Ratings and Reviews

If you have a product to sell, the above examples may not do much for you. You don't generate a lot of editorial content; you're not releasing new online software, or pushing a political candidate. You just want to encourage people to buy! Well, user ratings and reviews are for you.

Pioneered almost from its very start by Amazon.com, user reviews and ratings are an incredibly powerful tool. Today, if you want them on your site—and syndicated to the web at large—you don't have to pour into the effort the millions of bucks Amazon did. A number of ecommerce platforms are building the feature into their software, but for most businesses, the quickest and easiest approach is to bolt on a third-party service, the two most notable currently being PowerReviews and Bazaarvoice.

Both work roughly the same: users review your product qualitatively, give it an overall one-to-five star rating, which will be displayed on a tab on the product detail page. Your product page will invite visitors to review the product. Best practices are also to solicit product feedback via email, when you send customers their order confirmation and shipping confirmation emails.

Case studies on the positive impact of reviews and ratings are compelling:

- *77% of online shoppers* use reviews and ratings when purchasing (*JupiterResearch*, August 2006).[5]
- *Conversion rate more than doubled*, from 0.44% to 1.04% after the same product displayed its five-star rating (*Marketing Experiments Journal*).[6]
- Shoppers who browsed the Bass Pro Shops "Top Rated Products" page had a 59% *higher conversion rate* than the site average, and spent 16% more per order.[7]
- Shoppers who browsed the "Top Rated Products" page at Petco had a 49% *higher conversion rate*, and 63% larger AOV.[8]

Bazaarvoice's "Social Commerce Report 2007"[9] found that user-submitted product reviews and ratings boosted site traffic, sales conversion rates, and average order values. Among ecommerce retailers in the United States and Europe who deployed reviews and ratings tools, 77% reported upticks in traffic, 56% reported improved conversion, and 42% reported higher AOV.

Only 5% to 9% reported that ratings and reviews tools impacted their performance negatively—presumably because of the presence of negative feedback.

Reviews can also be a boon for your search-engine optimization efforts. Every time a customer rates one of your products, they create a new web page linking to your product. By the nature of user-created content, user reviews are conversational, informal, rich in the keywords searchers actually use, and often full of the kind of misspellings, slang, and colloquialisms that you as a brand-conscious marketer would never use—but which search-engine spiders gobble right up.

You can choose to syndicate your new product reviews out to RSS feeds and comparative shopping platforms like PowerReviews' Buzzillions, giving you additional exposure to web shoppers. Expect to see a lot of additional convergence between user-submitted reviews and comparative shopping. Both are growing fast and will drive an increasing share of your traffic.

But wait, you say! What if my customers say negative or flat-wrong things about my products or me? Three things:

1. The overwhelming majority of user comments—80% according to Bazaarvoice—are positive: four stars or better.
2. The world is full of folks with chips on their shoulder, and the online world amplifies it. Users know that. A negative review or two, among otherwise stellar ratings, will be discounted by most customers. Your willingness to display the good, the bad, and the ugly galvanizes your reputation as a trustworthy merchant.
3. Online review tools give you, the administrator, the ability to approve, disapprove, or edit submission. Routinely you'll delete postings that are duplicate, incomplete, profane, or incoherent.

Regarding that last point, use your editorial power wisely! Legitimate gripes that you deep-six from your site will inevitably bob up elsewhere on the web—BizRate, epinions, TripAdvisor, or all over the blogosphere—and in more virulent form. Use this customer-feedback loop not just as a feel-good pretense to tout your stuff. More powerfully, it's an avenue to connect with your customers, understanding not just what they love, but what may be frustrating or misleading to them. In my opinion it's fully ethical to take each rotten review as a customer service call-to-action: quickly solve the customer's problem. If you do, the customer will likely volunteer to retract or edit the nasty review.

And as the old chestnut of the customer-service industry goes, the customer who has a bad experience that you resolve wonderfully becomes a more loyal customer than the one who doesn't have a problem in the first place!

Conversion rates are higher on products with less than perfect reviews (fewer than five stars) than those without reviews at all, indicating that the customer feels that the product has been properly reviewed by other customers.

This isn't just about the product pages of your website. You should also leverage the value of customer-created ratings and reviews by:

- Using them in your email campaigns.
- Syndicating them as RSS feeds.

- Syndicating them to shopping portals (the third-party ratings-and-review tools are already cutting deals with comparative shopping sites, and you can expect more to come).

When using star-ratings and reviews in its emails, pet-supply retailer PETCO realized a 5× increase in click-through rates.

In A/B tests by Golfsmith, promotional emails that featured the star ratings, and reviews of top products drove 46% higher revenue per campaign. The take-away is that customers trust and respond well to the voices of their fellow customers. By transforming your marketing into a Web 2.0 customer-to-customer communication, you can tap into that trust and your results will benefit.

▪ Idea 3. Add Value for Customer Registration

When it comes to customer registration, we know what's in it for you, the marketer. By welcoming returning visitors and saving them from redundant data entry, you speed them through the checkout and improve your sales conversion rate. Many customers will give you permission to send email newsletters or promotions—a source of such dependable, high-ROI revenue that ecommerce merchants rank emails number one among their marketing mix.

But what's in it for the customer?

Today, a web user's personal data, and the permission to communicate with her by email, are more precious than ever. They must be respected. People don't grant permission lightly, and they have high standards for upholding your end of the relationship.

What are you offering that is so valuable, so efficient, or so entertaining to members? What makes it worth filling in several fields of personal information and trusting you to a relationship?

Remember, we live in an age of mushrooming personal online accounts, manifold usernames and passwords—one of the chief irritations of internet users today. Even stronger is customers' reluctance to expose themselves to unwanted emails, the risk of identity theft, and credit card fraud. With those four concerns working against you, what makes it compelling for visitors to register at your site?

The traditional, Web 1.0 arguments for member benefits are:

- Faster, more convenient checkout
- Access to your order history, and delivery address books
- Money-saving email offers or exclusive access to new or clearance products, etc.

These still should be part of your calculus—and you should be especially honest with yourself about that last item. Your email program must *really* treat members special. Offer discounts not available to the public at large; give sneak peeks, special gifts, white papers and other valuable research; invite members to participate in fun product research surveys or beta programs; segment and tailor the information in your messages as closely as possible to the needs of the recipients. When you create your email plan, think like a consumer, not a marketer, and come up with valuable and interesting messages that you'd appreciate receiving.

Beyond those basic benefits, build a worthwhile member experience into the fabric of your website. While Web 1.0 member features often didn't come into play until checkout, Web 2.0 sites present custom experiences based on the member's identity. Many sites today—including social network sites, reputation-driven sites like eBay, and subscription programs like Netflix and Blockbuster—simply can't be used without first creating a member profile. Examples of Web 2.0-style member registration include:

- Rich member profiles, including uploaded photos and other user-generated content.
- Ability for members to establish links to one another.
- Ability to rate and review past purchases.
- Online package tracking, returns and exchanges, and other customer services.
- Ability to maintain browsing and ordering history for a variety of purposes including wish lists, gift registries, corporate gift lists.
- Member-only forums, special interest groups, etc.
- Special member discounting, frequent-flyer miles, points generation, or other member incentives.

Ecommerce retailers, B2B sites, and others are taking the cue from social media. Whatever market you serve, it has its passionate adherents, people eager to rate products, share their favorites, and interact with other like-minded customers. Amazon members can establish profiles, link with friends, create and promote their book lists, and display all their reviews. Netflix members rate and review what they watch, and can see what their friends are watching and reviewing. Netflix, Yahoo! Radio, and other sites make better suggestions the more you use them.

I'm not suggesting you make a multimillion-dollar investment in custom recommendation engines and social media platforms. I'm suggesting you identify the features that most appeal to your customers, and deploy them—in many cases you can find the tools as third-party apps or already built into many web platforms. Have your website make suggestions based on the customer's categories of interest. If you can't do it algorithmically, based on past purchases, give them the option of telling you during the registration process. Imagine your website delivering dynamic content based, say, on whether a customer is interested in red wine or white, European vacations or Vegas.

Even if you don't customize the website experience based on customer interests, you can easily segment your email list to do so. That will inevitably improve the relevance of your emails, and better maintain your important permission-based relationship with the customer.

Finally, even after building all these compelling advantages into the idea of site registration, make it fast, easy, and encouraging! Netflix is a perfect example: visit the site without a member cookie on your computer, and the entire homepage is dedicated to capturing new signups. There's a huge call to action ("Sign up today and try Netflix for Free!") and a bare-bones signup form consisting of just four fields to get started. There are a few bullet points and clear graphics explaining how it works, and the basic plan price.

Your business may not be as strongly oriented toward member generation as that of Netflix—few businesses are! But the lesson remains: build authentic value into the member experience, and make it as easy as possible to sign up.

▓ Idea 4. Create Valuable Content and Set it Free

Anything new and newsworthy your organization does is worthy fodder for syndication outside the narrow confines of your own website. Send it out onto the custom homepages and feed-readers of your customers and prospects across the entire web. If you're not doing anything new and newsworthy, which would inspire someone to subscribe, give yourself a long, hard look! It's a basic Web 2.0 imperative that you offer something valuable and interesting enough to make at least your core audience request and anticipate it.

Use your imagination. Each season's new-product introductions can be suitable feed data. So can your daily blog posts, assuming they're relevant and of high quality. Newly discounted clearance-sale items, research reports, case studies, or even press releases (again, assuming they're truly newsworthy). Bestseller lists, new videos or music files, career opportunities, sports scores, industry events listings—these and other data are natural candidates for feeds.

You don't need the whole world to subscribe to your feeds to make it a valuable exercise. All you need is your core audience, perhaps within just a few important niches you serve, and your feed program will be a success. Why? Even if you're unable to tie a lot of revenue directly to these efforts, they are Web 2.0 best practice, for three reasons:

- You will connect with your best, most motivated customers on their own terms. They will inevitably be your company's biggest, most influential evangelists. Odds are, they will spread the word to prospective customers, other websites, perhaps even the media.
- You will be syndicating your content to the web, expanding your reach.
- You will benefit from the regular exercise of developing content that people will *ask to receive*, and actually look forward to seeing on their customized portal pages, readers, mobile devices, or elsewhere. When you start thinking harder about creating desirable information for your audience, it's a win-win.

The Power of APIs

Another pleasant side effect of open interfaces is the ecosystem of smart developers that springs up around your products, services, and data. For any business strapped for development resources, a smart web-services strategy can be a huge boon. If you can identify what's appealing about your data and how outside developers might want to interact with it, you can grow your reach across the web.

When you create valuable content, at some significant cost to your organization, it runs against your instincts to give it away. But Web 2.0 is about creating valuable content and setting it free. Why would you do that? Because when your valuable, interesting, timely data is being called by myriad different websites and mobile devices and feed readers—and perhaps being repurposed, or mashed up with Google Maps satellite imagery, Alexa traffic graphs, or other data—it ultimately creates more buzz and attention for your stuff. Websites link to you. Smart programmers develop cool tools that display your products or services in other contexts, from other perspectives, and drive business back to you.

Web services work both ways. It's a good idea to walk before you run: Before opening your own data to the world, set your developers loose on some of the great API toolsets out there from Google, Amazon, Yahoo!, Alexa, Facebook, and others. Chances are, you can add value to your own data for your visitors by overlaying it with third-party data that is available to you through an API interface. For instance, your retail locations, or the contact info for your regional salespeople, could be presented more engagingly if it were "mashed up" with publicly available maps, LinkedIn business networking relationships, or Twitter's data feed that describes where everyone is and what they're doing at the moment.

You needn't create a full-fledged, self-service API platform to explore whether your data is of interest to outside websites. You should first reach out to likely business partners: shopping sites that would like to display your daily bestseller lists, travel sites that might want to display your package tours, food sites that want to display your recipes, etc. By regularly exporting this data in XML format to the specifications of your partner, you'll get a feel for how it works, how much demand exists, and what's in it for you. That experience will tell you whether it makes sense to invest in API programming to share your data with the world.

▨ Idea 5. Enhance Your Branding and Security Messaging

Having worked on websites and shopped online since 1995, I have a somewhat jaded view of internet security—though I know the risks, I am generally confident about online shopping. However, a large majority of web users are preoccupied with the safety of their personal information and credit cards. *Fully 69% of customers say credit card security is a major concern when shopping online.*[10]

In addition to fearing identity theft and credit card fraud, people want to be assured about the quality of your company and its goods. If they purchase from you, they want assurances their privacy will be protected: Their address will not be sold to third parties, their email address won't be subject to spam.

These are not new concerns, but they are growing rather than abating. Why do I call them a Web 2.0 issue? Because today's online customers are more aware than ever about the potential risks of ecommerce, more protective than ever of their privacy, and faced with more alternatives—including trusted checkouts hosted by Google and PayPal.

Although innovative new sites are popping up at an ever-increasing rate, the Web 2.0 landscape is also one of consolidation. In most industries and niches, customers are less willing to take chances on unknown brands. Meanwhile, over the years, search has played an ever-larger role in helping prospective customers navigate. In addition to trying to make sense of all the "free" or organic search results, they have up to ten paid search ads to consider. Whether due to search engine algorithms, the herd mentality of ad copywriters, or the phenomenon of "dynamic keyword insertion" (automatic inclusion of your search term into the headline or body of an ad)—all those results can start looking alike. So today, in both your ad copy, meta description copy, and on your site, you need to work very hard to stand out, to communicate what your brand is all about, and why doing business with you beats that crowd of other alternatives.

Boost confidence about your brand and its practices. When customers consider doing business with you, they want to be assured of four things:

- You offer something special—the best, most, newest, or cheapest.
- If they're dissatisfied, for any reason, you offer a hassle-free, 100% guarantee.
- You'll respect their privacy, and not subject them to unwanted spam or junk mail.
- Their credit card and personal information is safe with you.

I have participated in a number of A/B tests measuring the impact of enhanced security messaging, in the form of the Hacker Safe seal—a logo that certifies a site, its database, and its servers have been scanned for potential vulnerabilities to hackers or credit card thieves. Depending on how well known is the brand, websites have experienced significant conversion rate lifts when displaying the Hacker Safe seal: 8% at Vermont Teddy Bear, 13% at PajamaGram, 12.8% at Yankee Candle, 8.8% at PETCO, 6% at Restoration Hardware, 5.2% at Cabela's.

I'll disclose here that my company, Timberline Interactive, is today a business partner of Hacker Safe, and we stand to make money when one of our customers uses the service. Hacker Safe was recently acquired by online security giant McAfee, which has begun branding its own "McAfee Secure" logo. And Hacker Safe is by no means the only logo to which customers respond in their quest for reassurance. Any of these can help establish trust and inspire visitors to complete a transaction:

- Verisign and other data-encryption seals on checkout.
- FedEx and UPS logos in your shipping info or checkout pages.
- Logos of the credit cards you accept.
- Your own 100% guarantee icon.

Finally, consider the role of the third-party checkouts, Google Checkout, and PayPal. These are quintessentially Web 2.0 responses to the problems of customer trust, and they consolidate a single customer account across many disparate websites.

Their disadvantages as payment methods are twofold: You lose some control over the customer relationship, and you lose some control over the checkout process. Their advantage: the customer recognition and trust enjoyed by the Google and PayPal brands.

▓ Idea 6. Deploy Web Analytics and A/B Testing

Web analytics software has really come of age. Whatever your budget, whatever level of staffing you can throw at analyzing and acting on the data, you have plenty of software offerings. And thanks to Google Analytics (the acquired and rechristened Urchin software), the price of good web stats program is now zero.

What has taken analytics into the Web 2.0 era is the availability of A/B and multivariate testing tools, which enable website owners to create a feedback loop between changes they make to their sites and the actual visitor response to them.

Another reason analytics is such a pressing Web 2.0 issue is that so many of the most popular types of content—streaming audio, videos, flash animations, page changes rendered by AJAX—fall outside the "page-view" counting on which traditional web analytics softwares were built.

All the major analytics platforms do have approaches for tracking all the abovementioned "events," but it can take some doing. And as managers we all need to have strategies for capturing the most important data. For instance, Nielsen/Netratings recently abandoned its longstanding page-view based rankings of websites, opting in favor of time-on-site measurements. The main instigation? Sites like YouTube, where the amount of time spent viewing videos is a more relevant stat than the number of different pages visited.

That same issue comes into play on rich AJAX sites, where any number of variations of content might be displayed, in response to user clicks, drags, and data entry, on what is, from a URL perspective, the same "page."

Today, tracking and A/B testing features are also built into a number of the online advertising networks, and into broadcast email programs as well. Stitching together all those stats packages so they convey an intelligible whole is a challenge, but the value of the data can be awesome.

▓ Idea 7. Segment Your Loyalty eMail Program

Online marketers are united in reporting that their in-house email program is their best performing online marketing tactic. Fully 80% of marketers in a Datran Media survey said so, with 82% planning to increase email spending in the coming year, and 55% expecting email ROI to be higher than any other online medium.[11]

Email delivers the highest ROI by an eye-popping margin: a whopping $57.25 for every dollar spent on it in 2005, according to the Direct Marketing Association.[12]

Yet despite the appeal of email marketing, few companies are applying personalization or other targeting—techniques that have proved their worth in other advertising media. Studies by *JupiterResearch* found that only 13% of marketers are using targeted email campaigns based on a customer's purchase history or click-stream activity.[13] Considering that your in-house email list represents your existing customers and other opt-in subscribers—people about whom you should have good, useful data—there's no excuse for ignoring that data to better target your email messages into relevant, useful, and effective campaigns. It's a win-win proposition.

Max Harris, Director of eCommerce at Gardener's Supply Company, provides an example. Rather than deliver recent customers a one-size-fits-all stream of messages, Gardeners.com is developing a program to customize some of its messages to the particular buying history of individual customers. Springtime buyers of its popular self-watering Tomato Success Kits, for instance, might receive follow-up messages tied to the life cycle of tomato gardening: fertilizer, replacement soil mix, pest control, climbing cage extensions—all targeted specifically to tomato-growers.

While your customer database already contains plenty of data to drive useful segments, it may be mute when it comes to valuable information about customer interests—data that a customer may be very happy to provide if you'd only ask them. So, while we're always at pains to limit the number of fields in a sign-up form, consider asking for segmentation data that would help you be a better emailer and your customer to be more satisfied. You might ask the customer to self-identify on different topics or interests, customer type (wholesale versus retail, say), and you can also ask the customer to specify how frequently they want to hear from you. When you segment your customers like this, generate unique email programs tailored to each, and you'll likely find they outperform your one-size-fits-all campaign.

eHobbies uses customer segmentation to great effect. On its newsletter sign-up form, checkboxes encourage customers to indicate their interest in Plastic Models, Radio Control, Rocketry, Slot Cars, or General. Targeted list-management like this can really transform the performance of an email program. "Segmentation has lifted our conversion by 40 percent," says eHobbies CEO Ken Kikkawa.[14]

In addition to segmenting your email program by customer demographic or product purchase history, think about *triggered emails*. We're all familiar with emails generated by *transactional triggers*: They're the order-confirmation or shipping confirmation messages generated a sale, or perhaps a "thanks for downloading our white paper," or "welcome to our newsletter." For the most part these are bland, text-only messages that take no advantage of their potential. Instead, view them as conversations with your most recent, most motivated, customers and prospects. Do something special, personal, and compelling to get recipients to take a next step with you, or be more positively disposed to reordering from you in the future. Give them a unique discount or free white paper. Extend an invitation to participate in a focus group, survey, or beta-testing community. Grant them access to a members-only sale, new product sneak-peek, or something else of real interest (to *them*, not just you!).

Not only are targeted emails more effective, and less likely to fatigue your customers into unsubscribing, but they also force you to think more personally about your audience. Personalizing the experience is what Web 2.0 is all about. When you start segmenting your email program, you'll also start viewing your website as a spectrum of distinct online experiences, each with their own characteristics and goals.

Great opportunities exist for triggering relevant email messages elsewhere in your relationship with your customers.

Sales Cycle Trigger is relevant in B2B and lead-generation businesses. Examples include new research white papers, new model year announcements from a car dealer, rate-triggered emails from your mortgage company about refinancing, or other messages that move leads along the process to purchase.

Event Triggers might be messages about conferences, seminars, webinars, or local store openings. Another triggering event many etailers now use effectively is the *customer event trigger*: a birthday, anniversary or other significant date (which must, of course, be stored in the merchant's customer database).

Membership Triggers are for new registered users of any website, members of subscription services, social media sites, etc. They are not limited to newly signed-up member confirmations, but are also effective ways to remind members of site upgrades, new policies, or updates occurring within their social network or groups they've joined. Membership triggers are the bread-and-butter for social media sites, which can use member news feeds to reach into the inbox to reel their members back onto the site.

Whatever your business, there are inevitably important triggering events that influence a customer's interest in your offerings. Picture the woman who goes from buying maternity wear, to nursing wear, to baby clothes. Or the financial services customer whose interests evolve from college loans, to a home mortgage, to retirement planning. Applying the power of database marketing to your email program will yield great fruit—in part because unlike print media, email can be sliced into quite small segments without running into prohibitive fixed costs.

The real attraction here is that by investing in really knowing your customers, and customizing messages that appeal directly to them, you create a win-win: you boost the performance of your program, reduce list churn from unsubscribes, and your customers don't feel bombarded by irrelevant messages.

Bill Nussey, CEO of Silverpop and author of the book, *The Quiet Revolution in Email Marketing*, acknowledges the biggest obstacle to launching segmented and triggered email programs is that they are time-consuming and complex, requiring investment in planning and management. "But companies should recognize that relevant, triggered emails deliver three to nine times the revenue of broadcast emails," Nussey says.[15]

Idea 8. Push Channel Integration

Marketers have for years been obsessing about their multichannel dilemma. How do you properly allocate sales, and come up with fair ROIs, when so many of your direct-marketing channels touch the same customer—and when the customer chooses between two major response channels, telephone and the web?

For example, say you're a longtime L.L. Bean customer. Bean sends you a catalog, which inspires you to go online. Rather than type the URL, you Google the company name and click on a paid search ad. You browse the site and find the argyle sweater you want, but you have a question about fit. You initiate an online customer-service chat and your question is answered. Now you're ready to order. Upon checking out, you see you can save a few bucks by having it delivered to the store, so you do.

All in all, it was a successful shopping experience for you, and for L.L. Bean, too. In the process you responded to two advertising campaigns (catalog and paid search), chose one response channel (the website), and called on two operational resources (online chat, and in-store delivery). How will Bean make sense of the relative value and cost of all those touchpoints?

Don't answer that, at least not right now. Sure, it's a valid question. But Web 2.0 challenges us to go even further in tearing down the walls. From a customer perspective, when choice is king, it's absolutely vital that merchants respond in whatever channel the customer prefers. As marketers, we want to get the customer to type in her catalog code. As ops people we face obstacles to allocating inventory to several different locations. But to a customer, it all needs to be seamless and utterly convenient. The last thing a customer wants to hear is that the color she wants is available only from the call center, or that her item can't be picked up in store, or that she has to read you her catalog code again.

The benefits of multichannel integration may be hard to quantify, but they are real. "Live chat has been a great initiative for us," points out eHobbies' Kikkawa. "It's hard to quantify increases attributed to it, but we know it's the right thing to do for our customers. We have been able to convert many customers through our chat function. It is difficult to tell whether these customers would have called or emailed us instead. But our philosophy is to make it as convenient as possible for our customers to contact us, by whatever way they choose."[16]

My advice for moving your multichannel operation further into Web 2.0 territory is to recognize that whatever makes it easy and flexible for the customer is best. You will have to develop some internal rules of thumb for allocating costs and sales to the various marketing pieces and CS touchpoints involved in a sale. Don't force your marketing, and the response to it, into silos. Embrace the multichannel nature of Web 2.0: Ensure your catalog and other marketing pieces prominently feature both your web address and 1-800 number, ensure that your website displays the phone number, and your call center hold message mentions the web address. Be liberal with alternate contact channels like online chat. Throw resources at your inventory system, so that the stores, the phone center, and the website all have pretty much the same product availability. Throw resources at pickup-in-store functionality, or backordering, or dropshipping. Use a key code system so that when customers enter their catalog number online, their name and address are autoentered. Offer a catalog quick-shop feature so that if visitors know exactly what SKUs they want, they can easily order them with one click.

▓ Idea 9. Position Yourself in Mobile Media

The mobile internet has been long predicted and slow to materialize, but web-enabled PDAs and cell phones are starting to reach critical mass in the United States. Not all of us have websites that will appeal to on-the-go customers. But many of us do—and almost all of us can identify a small subset of our most timely, local, or urgently needed products that would appeal to mobile users.

If you operate multiple retail locations, or if you products are distributed nationwide through certain outlets, local search is a no-brainer. Starbucks, for instance, launched a store-locator app for mobile devices. Walgreens has a mobile interface featuring a store finder, mobile-coupon signup, and more. Zagat offers its restaurant, hotel, resort, and golf course guides in a downloadable software for Palm, Blackberry, and other devices, or in a .mobi website for browsing on iPhones and other small web-enabled screens.

1-800 Flowers is a great example. Their principal website provides a typical online experience; they offer user registration and some personalized reminder services, but nothing especially Web 2.0. However, the company recently unveiled a site designed especially to handle transactions from cell phone and other mobile users, 1800flowers.mobi, which strips the site down to its bare bones: a handful of products and a quick credit-card checkout. Clearly what 1-800 Flowers has in mind is the busy, last-minute gift giver on a business trip the night before his or her spouse's birthday—someone who needs a gift, and a gift that he can order through his phone.

Other natural uses for mobile internet—and indeed the first players—are local retail, restaurant, and lodging businesses; also travel websites, and providers of information on sports, weather, and the markets.

Reserve the .mobi extension of your domain, even if you have no immediate plans for it.

At the time of writing this book, Google and Yahoo! are both testing mobile search ads in foreign markets, including Japan and India. The opportunity for U.S. marketers to kick the tires is no doubt near at hand. While I know of few companies building end-to-end mobile websites, mobile advertising, and limited mobile-formatted microsites—to accept contest entrants or support some other promotion—could be a good way to dip your toes in.

Barry Chu built the Yahoo! Content Match network before moving to Seattle-based mobile search and advertising platform Medio Systems. Medio has helped clients mount mobile search campaigns, both to send clicks to a WAP web page, or to generate phone leads with a click-to-call. Chu describes the mobile web opportunity this way: "Mobile is still in its pioneer days, and it is experiencing hockey-stick growth. But it is still very inexpensive to advertise in mobile search. The best time to learn is before your competitors do."[17]

The Michigan-based outdoor outfitter, Moosejaw, tested the mobile waters by asking customers to sign up for text messages and coupons. One text promotion sent to customers' handsets read: "Text me back with Rock, Paper or Scissors. I already know what I'm throwing, and if you beat me, I'll add 100 Moosejaw points to your account."

That mobile promotion achieved a 66% response rate, emboldening Moosejaw to commit to mobile commerce with a stripped-down .mobi ecommerce website, built on the mPoria m-commerce platform. Moosejaw.mobi makes the full 40,000-product inventory available for purchase through web-enabled PDAs and cell phones.[18] "Getting our Web site onto phones and doing text messaging are really important to us," says founder Robert Wolfe. "Our customers live on their phones, so we want to be there."

▦ Idea 10. Design Your Personal "Killer App"

Web 2.0 is about pushing the boundaries of what's possible. By now, surely, your main competitors and many new or smaller rivals already have websites, of varying quality, and are battling each other for the same keywords in paid search-engine advertising and in your efforts to rank well among the free, "organic" search results. You may be dueling each other with price cutting, and free shipping promotions. It looks like the same old, bruising competition, moved to a new arena.

But wait. Chances are, your industry or market niche is still awaiting its "killer app"—a new online tool (or "application," hence the "app") that solves customer needs in an innovative new way, or entertains or delights your audience at a whole new level.

What's the Killer App for your business? One that uses the new bandwidth, programming power, data processing, and social networking to really blow away your online customers. You want your online experience to be what Apple's Steve Jobs so famously calls "insanely great." But how?

Ironically, it doesn't have to be high-tech. When dreaming up the ideal online tool, it helps to brainstorm on both extremes: On one hand, picture how you'll use the rich, broadband, data-intensive, personalized, web experience that all the new technology makes possible to users of desktop or laptop computers. And on the other hand, ask yourself what is the most urgently needed kernel of information or service your customers want from you—and then picture it delivered across any of the new web-enabled cellphones, PDAs, and other devices. By necessity, for now, this latter type of killer app is going to be more narrowband, and designed in Spartan fashion to read well and be navigated easily on a small screen.

Scene7 founder, Doug Mack, points out a killer Web 2.0 app in the cell phone market: the German site Vodaphone.de. Its beautiful graphic "Handyfinder" interface dynamically reshuffles the product displays as you filter your product preferences (by price, and by features) until you are viewing only those phones that fit your criteria.

The killer app of the custom tee-shirt printing appears to be CustomInk.com's interface for viewing a custom tee-shirt design, with full user control over the style and color of the garment, plus full control over the art, message, font, and positioning of the design. It turns any web visitor into a graphic designer.

Not that they are the only company doing it: a number of rivals in the same field have similar interfaces. Because the barriers of technology and design on the web are getting lower and lower, a "killer app" is not likely to be worthy of its name anymore—it is not going to kill your rival businesses. But it will set the standard for customer satisfaction, should strongly benefit your key online business stats (like conversion rate, average order value, customer repeat rate, etc.), and give you a core around which to keep innovating and improving.

The killer app of Travelocity is the trip finder, the economical little calendar interface on its upper left NAV that lets you compare the best fares and schedules for a given itinerary. Again, all the other online travel sites and major airlines, eventually copied it, so it is not literally a competition-killer. But it has proven to be the standard for how customers cut to the chase when they visit a travel site. And the tool has spawned a number of variations that allow the players in the travel industry to satisfy customer needs and presumably gain some advantage over the other. Examples include the option to compare nearby airports, partner the flight reservation with rental car and/or lodging information, or search for the best price regardless of schedule.

Amazon.com's killer app is its affinity marketing engine—its ubiquitous "people who bought that also bought this"—and, in the same vein, its reliance on customer reviews and ratings, and customer-created lists or recommended products. The killer app for Zappos isn't an app at all, but its free shipping and free return-shipping policy, a marketing gesture that vaporizes the biggest obstacle for online shoe shoppers: what if they don't fit?

Think again of John Musser's vision of the "programmable web"—and picture that tidal wave of widgets washing across thousands upon thousands of different websites. Those phenomena remind us to view the web as a machine, one that is capable of running your own "killer app" as an easy, plug-in widget, everywhere interested web users are found.

7 ▪ ▪ ▪

The Dark Side: How the Latest Developments in Cyber Crime Can Ruin Your Day— Or Business

Online crime has long been with us, but the tactics and technologies are changing rapidly in an effort to stay a step ahead of the good guys. And the scope of recent cyber crimes is staggering. At least 45.7 million credit card and debit card numbers were stolen from TJX, owners of TJ Maxx, Marshall's, Homegoods, and other chains—the biggest known theft of credit card numbers in history. It started with hackers aiming a telescopic antenna at a Marshall's clothing store in Minnesota to snag unsecured wireless data beamed between cash registers, barcode scanners, and store computers. The hackers gained access to the parent company's central database, where for 18 months they helped themselves to card numbers and customer data.

- More than 40 million credit card numbers were accessed by a hacker using a SQL injection attack to breach the databases of CardSystems, Inc., a major card payment processor.
- Hackers seized email addresses and personal information of 1.3 million job seekers from Monster.com. They wasted no time before trying to turn the data into cash: Users received phishing emails inviting them to download a "Job Seeker Tool," which turned out to be a

Trojan Horse virus that promptly encrypted the files on the victim's computer. This was followed by an email "ransom note" demanding $300 for the files to be decrypted!

Cybercrime Glossary

Here's a brief glossary of hacking and cybercrime terms we'll continue hearing about:

ADWARE: Malicious programs that spawn popup ads in response to web browser behavior—visit any site and you'll see scads of rival popup ads, or URL addresses you type may be hijacked to compensate an affiliate.

BOT: A PC that has become infected with a worm or Trojan Horse virus, and been made a "robot" under the remote control of another.

BOTNET: A large number of virus-infected computers—sometimes tens of thousands—under the remote control of a single person using a command and control server. They may be used to generate fraudulent commissions, steal credit card data, relay spam emails, or launch a denial-of-service attack.

BOTNET HERDER: The controller of a botnet.

COMMAND and CONTROL: An IRC (Inter Relay Chat) server that communicates with a botnet and directs its actions, C & C for short.

CROSS-SITE SCRIPTING: An attack that injects code into a vulnerable website, such as a forum or dynamically generated page, to execute a malicious script. On execution, the script can capture data across different open browser windows on a user's computer. It's used, for instance, to steal credit card data or session cookie information from legitimate sites.

DRIVE-BY DOWNLOAD: Automatic installation of malicious code onto a visitor's PC, caused simply by visiting a "malware" website.

EXPLOIT: A software bug or vulnerability that hackers use to gain access to a computer, database, server, or network.

KEYLOGGER: An application installed on an infected machine to record every keystroke a user makes, for the purpose of capturing account numbers, passwords, or personal data. The data is relayed to a command-and-control machine for processing.

MALWARE: Any code used to maliciously exploit a system and gain control over it.

MALWARE WEBSITE: A website containing executable code capable of infecting a visitor's computer.

PHARMING: Redirecting a site's traffic to a bogus, malicious alternative.

PHISHING: Sending bogus emails that copy the look and feel of a bank, online service, or well-known company, to drive victims to a fake website and get them to give up credit card numbers, account information, or personal data. The scams may employ keylogging, or spawn well-known sites within an invisible frame. Phishing scams often target PayPal, Monster.com, Google Adwords, and Chase and other banks and credit card firms.

SESSION RIDING: An attack that causes a user to launch a new browser window, then takes advantage of the fact that a user is logged into a particular website—using the user's credentials to change passwords or access financial or personal information behind the scenes.

SPYWARE: A malicious program that captures personal information from an infected computer and sends it to a remote server.

SQL INJECTION ATTACK: An exploit of websites using SQL databases, in which the attacker adds SQL code to a form input field (it could be an inquiry form, a checkout page, etc.) to gain administrative access to the data or server.

TROJAN: A file that looks harmless but is actually an executable virus or worm. Originally spread as email attachments, Trojans can also be sent as files across chat systems, or Trojan code inserted into otherwise benign applications.

VIRUS: A malicious program that is self-replicating but must be launched by a host application on the infected computer.

WORM: A malicious program that is self-replicating and doesn't require any host application in order to execute.

ZOMBIE: Another name for a bot.

Dollar losses from ecommerce fraud were $3.6 billion in 2007, according to CyberSource.[1] That's up 18%—in other words, despite aggressive security measures, fraud is still growing just as fast as online sales as a whole, afflicting a steady 1.4% of all sales. Says Doug Schwegman, Cyber-Source director of customer and market intelligence: "The picture is one of merchants swimming harder against an accelerating current."

Microsoft's 2007 Security Intelligence Report[2] noted a 500% increase in malicious code used to install Trojans, password stealers, keyboard loggers, and other malware on users' systems. Some 31.6 million phishing scams were detected, up 150% over the previous period.

Whenever you and your workmates surf the web or check emails, your computers and network can be exposed to a number of malicious attachments, scripts, and other nasty stuff poised to ruin your day. Whether your machine starts spewing popup ads, or sending everyone in your email address book spam for Viagra and Cialis, it's a bummer for you personally. But what I'm interested in are the risks posed by cybercrime to a typical online business.

Cybercriminals could hurt a business in a multitude of ways:

- Hackers could steal your customer's credit card numbers, email address and identities, and start racking up unauthorized charges. And under PCI standards (Payment Card Industry Data Security Standard), your firm could be liable.
- Phishers could send phony emails and host lookalike websites using your company name, logos, and look and feel, to gain control over your customers' computers, and/or trick them into giving up their credit card numbers and other data.
- Scammers could join your affiliate program and start reaping sales commissions from you for fraudulent or highjacked transactions.
- Bot-herders can exploit security weaknesses on your web servers in order to use them to relay huge volumes of spam email.
- Though rare (because there's no money in it!) your site could be the victim of a "defacement" (hackers gaining access and changing content to indicate their feat) or a distributed denial of service (DDOS) attack. A DDOS floods a target website with visits from thousands of zombie computers, effectively bringing its web servers to their knees.

The indirect damage done to your business by cybercrime is huge, too. Visitors made nervous about online transactions are ever harder to convert to customers. Prospects bombarded by unrequested spam are less likely to sign up for your email newsletter.

▨ The Motives

Just as Watergate investigators were urged to follow the money, we should look at the revenue sources attracting fraudsters:

Credit card and identity theft

Hackers can use your website as a platform for infecting your visitors' computers. Once infected, PCs can be scanned for credit card or personal data, or browser behavior can be manipulated to generate fraudulent revenue.

In the quest for credit card data, hackers can also attack your website's database, or capture unencrypted data flowing across unsecured networks, including wireless networks. Once they have the cards, they can use them for transactions, or sell the numbers for a few hundred dollars apiece.

Affiliate sales commissions

Your affiliate program provides an incentive to other websites to refer sales to you. Say it's an 8% share of revenue. There are legions of good, honest affiliates out there, and they send you real customers. This is an industry segment that has taken real pains to police itself, and weed out scammers and parasites. But the temptations for fraudulent affiliates are large: Market research firm MarketingSherpa estimated that in 2006, affiliates earned $6.5 billion in commissions and bounties, worldwide.[3]

A number of frauds, adware, and bot-net activities attempt to redirect or hijack URLs to capture a commission on sales transacted on the infected machines. One small-time gambit is to sign up as an affiliate and then use one's own tracking link to make big purchases using stolen credit cards. Although the merchant will cancel the fraudulent transactions, he may neglect to process a chargeback for the affiliate commissions.

Revenue share from online ads

The "content networks" of Google, Yahoo!, and other players have successfully monetized all sorts of web pages. Google's AdSense program displays AdWords ads on third-party sites, sharing with the site owners upwards of 75% of the proceeds of each click. Who are these site owners? Most of them are fine, upstanding citizens—the big guys are household names, and the little guys are bloggers and the like. And again, the ad networks claim to be vigilant about combating fraud. But with so much money at stake, and the sheer size of the network of sites, bogus clicks are still a big issue here, too.

Here are a few examples of these kinds of crime:

For two years, a 19-year-old high school dropout in California named Jeanson James Ancheta controlled a botnet of thousands of zombie PCs, raking in $60,000 through the installation of malicious adware, which compensated him with affiliate sales commissions on transactions from the infected machines. He pleaded guilty to federal charges and had to forfeit the money—and his BMW.

Antivirus experts identified a new Trojan that exploits Google's AdSense ad-serving system. The virus infects user computers, then hijacks Google text ads on visited pages and replaces them with ads compensating the hacker. Security company BitDefender identified the virus as Trojan.Qhost.WU, and said it causes an infected computer's browser to read ads from a server at a "replacement address" instead of from Google.[4]

"This is a serious situation that damages users and webmasters alike," said Attila-Mihaly Balazs, a BitDefender virus analyst. "Webmasters are affected because the trojan takes away viewers and thus a possible money source from their websites." Also affected would be the original advertisers, who will lose the hoped-for clicks.

In a different take on the same idea, a worm called KMeth worm, which targeted Yahoo! Messenger users, redirected infected users to a website serving Google AdSense ads related to the medical condition, mesothelioma. At several dollars a click, mesothelioma is one of the most expensive search terms on the internet today, and the fraudsters aimed to cash in on a rev-share from those misdirected clicks.

How Web 2.0 Technology Worsens the Problem

Unfortunately, the technologies that make Web 2.0 interactive are also responsible for the spread of more viruses and malware. The more multimedia the web experience becomes, the more familiar we all become with installing browser plug-ins and toolbars, drivers, widgets, and applets. "To view this content requires the latest version of Flash." Or Shockwave, or any of the slew of other audio and video players out there. Using cool Web 2.0 applications like MMOGs often require you to install drivers and utilities. Many users are getting increasingly blasé about installing add-on applications—but we need to be more vigilant than ever about the source of such applications.

User-created content can pose risks to you, the site owner. It can also pose privacy and identity-theft risks to your users. Many shopping sites allow visitors to search for others' wish lists by name or email address. Unless sites take security precautions, scammers can bombard a wish-list search with known or manufactured email addresses, harvest a bunch of wish lists, and send personalized phishing scam emails promoting wished-for items.

Could your webcam be spying on you? In a blackmail scam, a man in Spain was arrested for unleashing a virus capable of taking over infected computers and cams to do just that.

It used to be (in the Web 1.0 world) that you were as safe as long as you didn't launch any dubious executables or open any suspicious attachments. But nowadays, malicious code can install itself in the background when you simply visit the wrong web page.

Here are a few Web 2.0 vulnerabilities:

- Malware web pages.
- Viruses spread among web-enabled cell phones.
- Hacking wireless networks and Bluetooth conversations.

Malware

Inspecting some 4.5 billion web pages, Google researchers found that about 450,000 could perform *drive-by downloads*—automatically installing malicious code on the computers of its visitors.[5]

Ironically, the search engines themselves present the most attractive breeding grounds for the spread of harmful software. Search engine optimization (SEO) is writing web page copy, structuring a web page, and obtaining links, all with the goal of ranking well in searches for particular keywords and phrases. But in late 2007, a huge black-hat SEO effort caused tens of thousands of malware pages to rank highly on the results pages at Google itself, for innocuous searches like "funny dog pictures."

"This is huge," said Alex Eckelberry, CEO of Sunbelt Software, of what he referred to as an SEO poisoning. "So far we've found 27 different domains, each with up to 1,499 pages. That's 40,000 possible pages."[6]

Also aiding the spread of malware is interactive Web 2.0 content such as video and browser widgets, pay-per-click advertising, and social network pages. Blogs, wikis, forums, photo sharing apps, and the like can be good places for attackers to post malicious code. If comments or other input fields accept HTML, the attacker can insert JavaScript exploit code. Once the malicious comment is posted, every visitor to that page is exposed to the attack.

In another angle, the websites of *The Economist*, Major League Baseball, and Canada.com unwittingly displayed Flash banner ads promoting phony antivirus software. When customers clicked the banners, a Trojan installed itself on their computers and started scanning for bank accounts, PINs, and other data. The culprits used Doubleclick's DART ad-serving technology, the engine that serves banners on thousands of popular websites, to distribute the malicious code.[7]

The surging popularity of widgets presents another vulnerability. When a widget is embedded in a site, it calls an external third-party script, which could be used to gain access to visitors' machines. "Widgets may be vulnerable to hacking," says Yuval Ben-Itzhak, CTO at Finjan Security.[8]

"Vulnerabilities in widgets and gadgets enable attackers to gain control of user machines, and should be developed with security in mind."

As free widget distribution pages proliferate, hackers have an incentive to create their own cool-looking gadgets that users will install on their blogs and profile pages, only to launch attacks on visitors' PCs. The multimillion-friend network power of the big social networks means that bad news travels *really* fast.

In the first few days of 2008, over a million Facebook users—a stunning 4% of the total Facebook population—downloaded a new "Secret Crush" widget, which actually required them to install the Zango adware/spyware package. Facebook members were notified "you have a secret crush," and prompted to install an astrology widget. Those who breezed through the lengthy disclaimer language and downloaded it soon found their machines spewing pop-up ads and tracking their every online movement.

After Facebook banished Secret Crush for violating its terms of service, the widget reportedly popped right back up with the name My Admirer. Facebook snuffed out Admirer, too, but the episode was a vivid reminder of how quickly widgets can appear, spread, and reappear under innocent new names.

Zango points out that its agreement doesn't hide the nature of its software, but online privacy advocates argue that disclaimer language alone is insufficient. In 2007, Zango settled an unrelated lawsuit with the FTC for $3 million. The FTC said of Zango: "They used unfair and deceptive methods to download adware and obstruct consumers from removing it, in violation of federal law."[9]

Cell Phone Viruses

The global web-enabled cell phone network is just now reaching an inflection point where it is vulnerable to widespread virus outbreaks. "Viruses and worms cannot infect large numbers of wireless devices until at least 30% of users commonly receive emails with attachments," say Gartner analysts John Pescatore and John Girard.[10] We are now quickly approaching that level. "Once smartphones account for 30% of all wireless telephones in use," they say, "rapidly spreading attacks will be much more likely."

Analysts at IDC estimated that the global market for mobile phone security software will reach $1 billion in 2008.[11] But Gartner's Pescatore and Girard said: "The mobile world should not repeat the mistakes of the PC world. Malware protection services should be built into the network first, and device-side protection should be the last resort."

Wireless Hacking

Wireless networks carry an ever-increasing share of our important data transmission. The TJX debacle is lesson enough about the stakes in securing these wireless LANs (Local Area Networks) and WANs (Wide Area Networks). When data streams through the air—from PDAs to computers, between Bluetooth headsets, from a barcode scanner to a wireless cash register—if it's not well encrypted and the networks properly passworded, it can fall prey to hackers, business rivals, or the general public.

An early Bluetooth phone headset hack enabled anybody with a directional antenna and some "Car Whisperer" software to eavesdrop on conversations within 300 feet—and actually chime into them—assuming the security key had not been changed from the default.

There's even peril in the few inches separating your wireless keyboard and mouse from your computer. Two Swiss researchers recently used a radio receiver, soundcard, and software to snatch data flowing between a non-Bluetooth keyboard and its PC. Max Moser and Phillipp Schrodel of security firm Dreamlab Technologies warned that cybercriminals could employ similar attacks to log keystrokes and capture logins to online banking accounts and other sensitive data.[12] Moser and Schrodel were able to pick up and decrypt the data from a distance of 30 feet.

"Wireless communication is only as secure as the encryption technology used," said Moser. "Due to its nature, it can be tapped with little effort."

▓ What to Do?

My best advice for marketers and businesspeople is to be aware that Web 2.0 is afflicted with many of the "Wild West" qualities of Web 1.0—and they're fancier and more interactive than ever.

Internet security is unlikely to be the direct responsibility of readers of this book. Governments, security software and antivirus companies, spam filter technologies, and IT departments everywhere have been battling these kinds of threats for over a decade, and their white hat efforts will continue.

The credit card companies introduced a stringent Payment Card Industry Data Security Standard (PCI for short) that will make things tougher for hackers. The PCI standard mandates firewall and antivirus software, and regularly updated virus definitions. It requires companies to strongly encrypt data, to restrict which of your employees have access to customer credit card data, and to assign a unique identifying number to employees with that access. In addition, it governs monitoring of who views and downloads data, and periodic security system checks.

Security experts predict increasing attacks on Mac hardware, thanks largely to the spread of iPods and iPhones. For now, though, most of these ills principally afflict PCs running Microsoft operating systems and applications. But it is prudent to consider that any new foray into wireless devices, mobile, and PDA will face some novel cybercrime angles of their own.

Here are just a few priorities to bear in mind:

- Comply to PCI standards.
- Engage with leading security firms like Verisign and HackerSafe to ensure your website, its server, and database are protected from known vulnerabilities.
- If your website supports user-generated content, widgets, forums, etc., be certain that it accepts only text or very basic HTML—and refuses JavaScript and other executable code.
- Ensure credit cards authorize and settle before shipping any products. Investigate all credit card fraud, including the referring URL.
- Scrutinize how and where your affiliate partners appear. Carefully review their traffic, sales, and commissions. If sudden, large sales from a new partner seem too good to be true, they probably are.
- If you distribute your text ads across a content network, review your stats for large traffic flows that didn't result in any sales. It could be click-fraud designed to line the pocket of a site owner.

8 ▪ ▪ ▪

Web 3.0: What Does the Future Hold?

As soon as we all started calling today's cutting edge "Web 2.0," the technorati had to identify the "new, new thing" and christen it Web 3.0.

So what is Web 3.0 going to look like?

To be worthy of a whole new version number, Web 3.0 needs to represent a real quantum leap—not just "more" of all the things we already think of as Web 2.0 (e.g., more bandwidth, more rich media, more social networking).

Already, a number of trends stand at the margins of our current online experience that promise to remake the web in dramatic ways—solving inefficiencies we now take for granted, immersing us in powerful entertainment and effortless communication, and opening up new possibilities that are really the stuff of science fiction. To borrow the words of that master of science fiction, Arthur C. Clarke: "Any sufficiently advanced technology is indistinguishable from magic."

To get the broad view, it's helpful to hear what some of the web's visionaries have to say on the subject:

> People keep asking what Web 3.0 is. I think maybe when you've got an overlay of scalable vector graphics—everything rippling and

folding and looking misty—on Web 2.0, and access to a Semantic Web integrated across a huge space of data, you'll have access to an unbelievable data resource. (Tim Berners-Lee, founder of the World Wide Web)[1]

Web 1.0 was dial-up, 50K average bandwidth, Web 2.0 is an average 1 megabit of bandwidth and Web 3.0 will be 10 megabits of bandwidth all the time, which will be the full video web, and that will feel like Web 3.0. (Reed Hastings, Netflix founder and CEO)[2]

Web 2.0 is well-documented and talked about. The power of the Net reached a critical mass, with capabilities that can be done on a network level. We are also seeing richer devices over the last four years and richer ways of interacting with the network, not only in hardware like game consoles and mobile devices, but also in the software layer. You don't have to be a computer scientist to create a program. We are seeing that manifest in Web 2.0, and 3.0 will be a great extension of that, a true communal medium . . . the distinction between professional, semi-professional and consumers will get blurred, creating a network effect of business and applications. (Jerry Yang, Yahoo! cofounder)[3]

Web 3.0 is a return to what was great about media and technology before Web 2.0: recognizing talent and expertise, the ownership of one's words, and fairness. (Jason Calacanis, founder of the wiki-edited search engine, Mahalo)[4]

[Web 3.0 will be] applications that are pieced together, with the characteristics that the apps are relatively small, the data is in the cloud, the apps can run on any device, PC or mobile. The apps are very fast and very customizable, and are distributed virally [via] social networks, email, etc. (Eric Schmidt, Google CEO)[5]

The five trends and technologies I see at the vanguard of Web 3.0 are:

- The Semantic Web and Artificial Intelligence
- Cloud computing
- Universal, portable, and online identities
- 3-D internet
- True convergence of web, mobile devices, and other equipment

The Semantic Web and Artificial Intelligence

Web 1.0 was a web of interconnected documents. The documents were produced to be read and understood by people.

Web 2.0 makes database calls and produces dynamic web pages customized to reflect the particular data that was requested, its combinations and options, and in many cases the identity, preferences, and referring URL of the particular web user.

But even before the first iteration of the web was catching on with the general public, its inventor, Tim Berners-Lee, was mindful of the shortcomings of a web of interconnected documents, and he sketched the theoretical and technical underpinnings of a new, smarter web—a web of meaning—to be layered over the old. He called this the Semantic Web.

In Web 3.0, the Semantic Web will use the global network of computers to exchange data about the data—in other words, metadata—to deliver more than simple documents. At a fundamental level, Web 3.0 will enable computers to "know" what a particular query means, and to know what particular documents and data are about, and to know the relationships between it all.

The Semantic Web introduced a logical language that human programmers could use to inform computers of the relationships between data—with the goal of replacing the old "web of links" with a new "web of meaning." Though the Semantic Web sounds like Artificial Intelligence (AI), Berners-Lee argues that is not its intent:

> The concept of machine-understandable documents does not imply some magical artificial intelligence, which allows machines to comprehend human mumblings. It only indicates a machine's ability to solve a well-defined problem by performing well-defined operations on existing well-defined data. Instead of asking machines to understand people's language, it involves asking people to make the extra effort.[6]

In the late 1990s, when Tim Berners-Lee began talking about the Semantic Web, he said:

> I have a dream for the web [in which computers] become capable of analyzing all the data on the web—the content, links, and transactions between people and computers. A "Semantic Web," which should make this possible, has yet to emerge, but when it does, the day-to-day mechanisms of trade, bureaucracy, and our daily lives will be handled by machines talking to machines. The

"intelligent agents" people have touted for ages will finally materialize.

If HTML and the web made all the online documents look like one huge book, RDF, schema, and inference languages will make all the data in the world look like one huge database.[7]

The Semantic Web is envisioned as a network that is able to describe things in a way that computers can understand, by structuring data into fields and defining the properties of things (like dimensions, prices, age, location) and the relationships between things (one entity is a member of another).

To date, the particular structure and standards Tim Berners-Lee laid out for the Semantic Web haven't really caught on, but they have inspired both top-down and bottom-up approaches. Many of the Web 2.0 technologies we've talked about—from APIs and data mashups to the open "social graph" standard promulgated by Google—have accomplished the same goal as put forth in the Semantic Web initiative. That is, they have produced structured data, and added a layer of logic, or metadata (information about information), to help disparate websites interact with the same content in myriad ways, all of them different but all of them meaningful.

Meanwhile, human-powered tagging, as practiced by del.icio.us, Flickr, and other sites, has provided a rich source of semantic intelligence, giving structure to previously unstructured data. Google Base is another example of an attempt to capture structured data in an online form—but since it is walled-off from other content online, it's of limited usefulness. The most promising Semantic Web tools today, including Twine, Spock, and others, rely on user tagging and other social-networking practices, as well as traditional web-crawling, to build a smarter layer for the internet. Twine, for instance, automatically learns about its users and their interests as they populate it with content, creating a "Semantic Graph." But it's not all user-generated. Twine has developed a "machine learning" approach that scours Wikipedia to "learn" about new concepts.

Web software architect and entrepreneur Alex Iskold wrote on Read-WriteWeb that today's web services (and even the screen-scraping programs that harvest and structure data from websites that lack web services) are the precursors of a true Semantic Web:

Today's web has terabytes of information available to humans, but hidden from computers. It is a paradox that information is stuck inside HTML pages, formatted in esoteric ways that are difficult for machines to process. The so-called Web 3.0, which is likely to be a precursor of the real Semantic Web, is going to change this. What we mean by "Web 3.0" is that major websites are going to be transformed into web services—and will effectively expose their information to the world.[8]

"The net effect," adds Iskold, "will be that unstructured information will give way to structured information—paving the road to more intelligent computing."

Berners-Lee was clear that the Semantic Web shouldn't be confused with Artificial Intelligence. However, many AI researchers do now view the web as an important frontier for their field. The distributed computing power of the web, and its organic interconnectedness, bear some similarities to the structure of the brain. Because the web is such a vast storehouse of information, much of it text, the web is a great testing ground for linguistic Artificial Intelligence. Some of the earliest efforts, like the Ask Jeeves natural-language search engine, were failures. Rather than teaching machines to respond to human speech patterns and "talk" like humans, over the past 10 years humans have instead become trained to talk like machines—typing search queries in ungrammatical strings of keywords, quotation marks, and Boolean operators. Still, all the major search engines can be seen as Artificial Intelligence at work: They are effective at parsing human queries and returning relevant "answers" in the form of search results.

The most famous description of Artificial Intelligence is the Turing Test, named for Alex Turing, who proposed it in 1950. A computer or other machine could be said to have achieved Artificial Intelligence when a human judge could mistake its responses for those of a human. Today, narrowly defined "expert systems" and algorithmic problem-solving applications like supercomputer chess programs can easily trump the human experts. But the Turing Test, based as it is on a devilishly simple but boundless definition of human intelligence, has proven a very hard standard to meet. AI researchers generally devise systems to take on particular facets of human intellect: understanding language, visual recognition, learning, reasoning, problem solving, etc.

The web offers a number of fun AI "chatbots," which, although diverting, demonstrate how far there is yet to go before an AI program can convincingly approximate human communication. But these and other web-driven AI projects are harnessing human input to help teach the systems to be more convincingly human. For instance, some chatbots encourage human users to correct the bot when its responses are off the mark (corrections are saved into the database to be used when similar discussions occur in the future). A user can also tip off the computer as to the emotional tone of each post, or his or her emotional reaction—from agreement to fury, sympathy to bafflement—to each bot response.

Artificial Intelligence is already at work on the web in more prosaic but more successful forms. Email spam filters use data-crunching machine intelligence to discriminate spam from desirable email. Data analysis engines flag potential credit card fraud or identity theft. In the future they will be able to do all that and more, identifying your interests, travel patterns, and spending habits and noting when your behavior diverges from the norm.

AI is present in many computer games, perhaps most notably in simulated worlds, or sims—where societies, economies, armies, zoos, and other complex systems arise, develop, and often collapse based on algorithms governing the health and growth of each element of the system. Villains and nonplayer characters owe much of their behavior to artificial intelligence—what they do and say is governed not by a strict script for a few scenarios, but by a series of logical rules, algorithms, and heuristics (rules of thumb for solving particular problems) ranging from pathfinding, verbal responses, strategies, etc.

Where Web 3.0 will likely deliver the most useful Artificial Intelligence will be in well-defined contexts. For instance:

- Harnessed to a rich enough database of FAQs and expert answers, friendly text-to-speech avatars could finally produce a truly helpful, interactive, automated customer support system.
- Predictive search engines, shopping engines, and other tools will already know what you're likely to want based on your past history. What they can't serve up to you based on your cookies alone, they'll start serving you up the most likely results based on your first few keystrokes and mouse clicks.
- Recommendation Engines like those used by Netflix and Yahoo! Radio will spread to the web at large. Merchants and content providers will better understand the affinities among their offerings, and thanks to your database of prior ratings, and your similarities to other users whose ratings reveal similar tastes, they'll know how to make suggestions likely to appeal to you. Thanks to flowering social networks, sites will be able to intuit a great deal about your interests based on the social circle of which you're a part.

Meanwhile, in a nice ironic twist, some companies are using the web's network effect to leverage human intelligence. Amazon's Mechanical Turk is a somewhat tongue-in-cheek take on the eighteenth-century mechanical chess player of the same name (the original was a hoax—a motorized figure controlled by an actual human chess player hidden inside). Dubbed "Artificial Artificial Intelligence," Amazon's Turk system lets posters pay humans small amounts to perform posted HITs or "human intelligence tasks," like reviewing a product, making a prediction, answering a question, etc. Likewise, Google Image Labeler fulfills a need for keyword tags to help drive its image search, by inventing a multiplayer image-tagging game.

The Web 2.0-style search engine Mahalo, which we mentioned earlier in the book, is another good example of the fusion of machine and human intelligence. Strictly human-edited, Web 1.0 approaches like Yahoo! Directory and dMoz failed to scale, unable to keep pace with the exponentially growing web. Founder and CEO Jason Calacanis describes the Mahalo strategy as threefold. First, the high-profile, frequently searched "head terms" will be the work of human intelligence—a network of trusted editors ("one of the largest distributed workforces on the planet"). Then, the "long tail" of search is filled in by machine intelligence (in the case of Mahalo, syndicating the Google results set). In the middle, the "mid terms" will be the product of social networking: an army of interconnected people, related to each other in a social network, reporting on their tastes and interests, and rated for the quality of the links they submit and rank.

The bottom line: the web is growing ever smarter. It is an unprecedented network of computing power and human feedback. Developers are working to make all those connected machines "understand" the nature of the data hosted on the network. They're also building in human intelligence, through rating, ranking, labeling, tagging, and sorting the data that the computers serve up. Increasingly, the web will be programmed to be self-perfecting—to learn from experience, and from the human feedback of a web population now numbering over a billion people worldwide.

Cloud Computing

Google won't reveal how many servers power its business—estimates go as high as a *million* networked machines—but they represent a key asset that the company plans to leverage in new ways. CEO Eric Schmidt has often described his vision of "Cloud Computing." Google and others will offer all their massive computing power, governed by what he calls the Internet Operating System, to businesses all over the globe in place of traditional software.

This isn't fundamentally different from the Software-as-a-Service (SaaS) model we discussed earlier, except in its scope. Basically, Cloud Computing advocates envision a future without packaged software, without costly software licenses, a future where all the computer resources and application development you need can be found, like a public utility, on the web.

In the Google vision, the services would be free, underwritten by targeted advertising, and perhaps with fees to power-users.

Picture the internet not as a web of separate devices, but as a massive supercomputer. The network of distributed computing power, and of limitless data storage, is the cloud—a resource "out there" that individual users and businesses could harness on demand. Local data storage, and installing expensive software on your own PC or LAN, could become things of the past.

Google has partnered with IBM in a Cloud Computing project for academia, and IBM has rolled out its Blue Cloud approach to businesses and governments as a sort of mini-internet, for running IT environments and developing and testing large-scale Web 2.0 applications, for instance. IBM's cloud will help clients build, test, and scale-up "large pools of systems" and integrate data-intensive Web 2.0 applications such as mashups, open collaboration, social networking, and mobile commerce.

"Blue Cloud will help our customers quickly establish a cloud-computing environment to test and prototype Web 2.0 applications within their enterprise environment," said Rod Adkins, Senior Vice President, Development and Manufacturing for IBM Systems & Technology Group.[9]

Meanwhile, Yahoo! has rolled out its own cloud, a cluster of servers dubbed "M45," after a star cluster of the same name. In a joint project with Carnegie Mellon, Yahoo! aims to support research into web-scale distributed computing. The M45 cloud functions as one of the fifty fastest supercomputers in the world, capable of processing speeds of twenty-seven Teraflops.[10]

"Yahoo! is dedicated to working with leading universities to solve some of the most critical computing challenges facing our industry," said Ron Brachman, vice president and head of Yahoo! academic relations. "Launching this program and M45 is a significant milestone in creating a global, collaborative research community working to advance the new sciences of the internet."

▪ Universal, Portable, Online Identities

We've already touched on the multiplicity of different online accounts, each with their own usernames and passwords, which currently clutter our lives. A number of competing services and standards have arisen to try to solve that problem, streamline your web experience, and consolidate your online identities. In Web 3.0, you'll largely be able to carry your identity with you from site to site without establishing accounts at each and every place you socialize, search, or do business.

The battle for who will control your universal online account is a heated one, and there will likely be a number of winners. Google Checkout and PayPal have staked their claims to the ecommerce shopping cart, storing your personal data and credit card information and then offering an alternate checkout path on thousands of commerce websites. (Yahoo! Wallet is seldom mentioned in the same breath as these, probably because it is useful only across Yahoo! Stores and Yahoo! Properties, but has no platform for implementation on non-Yahoo! Sites.)

The major portal companies, Yahoo!, MSN, and Google, have poured effort into unifying your account across all their properties. Google lets you personalize your search history, manage your paid search advertising, monitor your website's Google Analytics data, check on your email, communicate by IM, participate in groups, develop mashups, share and rate YouTube videos, and more, all with a single account. MSN and Yahoo! have been equally focused on unifying communication tools, online advertising, entertainment, and personalized homepages. Within vertical niches like financial services, the major mutual fund companies and brokerage firms have made moves toward facilitating single, integrated accounts for all your assets regardless of where they're held. TurboTax integrates its software across the web with statements from your financial accounts, your payroll accounting system at work, and last year's filing data saved locally or using their online software-as-a-service—all to make this year's filing as consolidated and automatic as can be.

But these are proprietary platforms, which can be expected to jealously guard their installed base rather than share their accounts (as an open standard), with each other. OpenID is a more grassroots, not-for-profit initiative. It's accepted by Technorati, Plaxo, Wetpaint, and other groovy, open-minded 2.0 sites, but the sad fact is, the value of a universal ID is all about adoption: Until your OpenID is accepted everywhere, it won't be accepted anywhere! That said, at the time of writing this book, Yahoo!, MSN, and Google are all talking about supporting OpenID as a standard.

Increasingly, we'll see tools spring up for migrating your profile from one social networking site to another. These powers should rest in the hands of users, not the services themselves. Currently, in the new-member registration process, social media sites have gotten eerily aggressive asking you (sometimes in fine print) to harvest potential "friends" from your Gmail, LinkedIn, Outlook, or other contacts. If you breeze through the signup process, you can belatedly find that the system has, in your name, spammed all your personal email accounts to urge them to join the site.

Synchronization of information across disconnected sites will be a great area of opportunity. For example, Trillian, an instant message aggregator, will connect all your IM services and their contacts into one.

Google established its OpenSocial standard for the social graph—social networking profiles and friends lists—so that you can port your identity, and your network of friends, from one social media website to many others including Engage, Friendster, hi5, Hyves, imeem, LinkedIn, MySpace, Ning, Oracle, Orkut, Plaxo, Salesforce.com, and Six Apart.

Now, even your avatar is being groomed for convergence: IBM and "SecondLife" developer Linden Lab have undertaken a joint project to develop a universal avatar that you can take from one virtual world to another.[11]

"When you talk about avatars going in and out of virtual worlds, we truly believe that expands the market," said Ginsu Yoon, vice president of business affairs at Linden Lab. "It's not a situation where there is a fixed pie and everyone is fighting for slices. It's really key to making the market bigger."

Convergence would likely consist of a single avatar, which would have the same appearance and characteristics, identity, and login credentials, across a number of virtual worlds. Integrated worlds would allow players to teleport between them, and fetch items belonging to them. That said, the limitations to totally open virtual-world platforms are obvious: Bodacious babes and hunks from Second Life are never going to be seamlessly integrated into Club Penguin!

By "universal" I'm not suggesting that future web-users will be stuck with presenting a single image or identity to the people with whom they interact online. They will surely have to option to maintain an entire portfolio of identities and looks appropriate to whatever virtual world, social network, or transactional environment they enter.

Another means we'll carry our identities with us will be the increasing role played by behavioral targeting. The ad networks that already serve well over 80% of web visitors have a few goals: (1) identify visitors and their likely interests via cookies; (2) serve them relevant ads; and (3) drive them to the websites of paying advertisers. In turn, those paying advertisers have much to gain by recognizing their visitors personally and serving them personalized, custom content. While identity recognition has in the past depended mostly on cookies, in the future we'll see cookies working in tandem with other methods for recognition, for instance:

- IP-based recognition, where a website knows your geographical location and can serve local ads, local weather reports—even make assumptions about your household income.
- ISP-driven tracking, where an internet service provider delivers information about you to advertising sites for the purpose of driving targeted advertising.

- Data mining: combining and cross-referencing individual bits of data you provide (your email address or name) with bits of data you don't provide but can be detected (IP address for instance), and matching postal address and other public database information.

Going further into the future, we'll be spared typing our contact information, address book, credit card information, and the like every time we shop at a new site. Whether using locally installed software that remembers form data for us, or wirelessly zapping our payment and address data from our cell phones to mobile websites, we will have much more convenient (but still secure) means to transfer our data to the sites with which we do business.

The bottom line is that, both for our own convenience and to feather the pockets of advertisers, the web of the future is generally going to know who we are, and require us to do relatively little typing to introduce ourselves and open our wallets.

▪ 3-D Internet

"The passage from 2-D to 3-D on the web as well as the virtual identity is the next big thing," Louise Guay, founder of MyVirtualModel, told *Fortune* magazine.[12]

With full broadband adoption, and advances in virtual worlds programming, we can expect to travel through colorful, realistic 3-D-seeming spaces when we navigate the web. If we wish, we will be represented by avatars wherever we go online, and we'll interact with the avatars of merchants, professors, colleagues, and fellow web users.

At a 2007 MIT Media Lab conference on "Virtual Worlds: Where Business, Society, Technology & Policy Converge,"[13] lab director Frank Moss said society is at the very beginning of something very big: "The first minutes, perhaps seconds, of the 3-D internet."

Web entrepreneur and blogger Dirk Knemeyer tells us that people use the internet for four basic purposes: to trade, to connect, to feel, and to learn. And at least two of those activities—feeling and connecting—are best suited to 3-D and real-time feedback. Entertainment and personal interaction are naturals for virtual reality.

With avatars, virtual worlds, vector graphics, and streaming media, the notion of the web as flat "pages" is changing. Text-typing and mouse-click navigation are not in danger of becoming extinct, but new methods of interaction with the web are more dynamic, and better suited to many applications and users.

Generation Y may have brought text messaging to an art form, but Web 3.0 will be a much richer and expressive communication medium. Today's webcams and video conferencing, streaming audio and VOIP, and 3-D avatars give us an idea of the more intuitive, interactive, online future.

Business conferencing will drive much of the improvements in streaming video and audio meetings. The real innovations will likely be ushered in by gaming technology. Take Nintendo's successful Wii motion-driven game console. The Wii's motion-sensing remote was not only a hit with the expected gamer audience, but also with senior citizens in retirement enclaves, and even nursing homes nationwide, who found the bowling and tennis games, for instance, fun and intuitive ways to get real exercise. These "silver surfers" and their Gen Y grandkids are the vanguard of demand for a richer variety of controllers and input devices. Digital imaging company 3-DV Systems has introduced a product it calls the ZCam, a webcam that is so sensitive to motion that players can control on-screen action by the merest of hand gestures.

Emotiv Systems, a San Francisco-based brain research and technology company, has an even loftier ambition: it aims to let you control your computer with your *mind*.

The initial aim for Emotiv's headset and application platform is to allow computer game players to manipulate objects in the game using the power of their thoughts.[14] The technology allows a computer to differentiate between particular thoughts such as lifting a displayed object or rotating it. The company says its technology can also detect and mimic a user's facial expressions, such as a smile or wink, and respond to emotions such as excitement or calmness—potentially reflecting the player's expressions on the face of her avatar.

In the future, Emotiv envisions its technology being applied to numerous industries, including interactive television, accessibility design, market research, medicine, and security.

"The next major wave of technology innovation will change the way humans interact with computers," says Nam Do, Emotiv cofounder and CEO. "As the massive adoption of concepts such as social networking and virtual worlds has proven, we are incorporating computer-based activities not only into the way we work, learn, and communicate, but also into the way we relax, socialize, and entertain ourselves. The next step is to enhance these experiences by making the way we interact with computers more lifelike."

In June 2008, researchers at Japan's Keio University unveiled a brain-computer-interface (BCI) that enabled a paralyzed man to move a SecondLife avatar—using nothing but his imagination.

The 41-year-old—unable to move his legs, and barely able to move his fingers—was fitted with three electrodes to detect brain activity associated with leg and hand motions. By imagining he was walking, the subject was actually able to manipulate his character through SecondLife's virtual world.

Keio faculty is also experimenting with devices that would let people compose text messages merely by visualizing the letters.[15]

Add to those futuristic input devices the existing text-to-speech interfaces like Oddcast, and touch-screen technology pioneered for PDAs and web-enabled phones, and you can see a wholesale change in the type-and-click model for navigating the web. We'll be able to interact with Web 3.0 environments more and more intuitively and comfortably just by speaking, moving, screen-tapping, capturing data with portable scanners, and zapping it between devices wirelessly.

Speaking of portable devices, they're the playing ground of the last major Web 3.0 trend we'll discuss.

True Convergence of Web and Mobile Devices

Take the interconnectedness of the web, the wireless convenience of portable devices, and the power of GPS, and you've got a potent combination.

At the 2008 World Economic Forum in Davos, Switzerland,[16] Google CEO Eric Schmidt called the emergence of a truly mobile Web a "huge revolution," one that is both huge in scope and imminent in timing: "It's the recreation of the internet, it's the recreation of the PC story and it is before us—and it is very likely it will happen in the next year."

Fully web-enabled cell phones and PDAs will offer a slew of integrated features to bring the mobile web to full fruition. Cell phones already support a vast arsenal of entertainment between your phone, principal email client, and your friends in MySpace, Facebook, LinkedIn, and all the other social networks in which you participate. You'll have always-on, wireless web connectivity to support your text messaging, emailing, video sharing, web browsing, Twitter, and other social network newsfeed alerts, local maps, and alerts driven by GPS tracking. Your phone's camera would be hooked into your Flickr and other photo sharing services; the video function will integrate with YouTube. Phones equipped with GPS will offer voice turn-by-turn directions, and use your location to serve localized search results, maps, and even alert you to the presence of nearby friends in your social networks.

We can expect much of the innovation of Web 3.0 to come from mobile devices. John Battelle describes a not-too-distant future where cell phones and PDAs could combine barcode scanners with online local-search for the killer app: Picture yourself shopping at your local Whole Foods supermarket and contemplating a pricey $52 bottle of Merlot. Not sure you're ready to part with that much cash, you discreetly use your phone to wand the barcode on the label, then submit it to a web-based local product search. Instantly, you're returned price comparisons and other data points telling you who else is selling the same bottle in the same neighborhood for how much—as well as alternate selections you might enjoy.

> *You click on the "list of prices at nearby stores" and see that the liquor store up the street is selling the same bottle for $39. You click on that store's link, and then choose the "reserve this item for same day pick up" option. With a satisfied smirk, you replace the bottle on its perch on the top shelf...* [17]

In-phone barcode scanners are not yet a reality in the U.S. market, but a well-established system exists in Japan, where cell phone users can employ the camera to scan barcodes present in print advertising, billboards, and other media, which contain contact info, website URLs, or online sign-up forms.

Soon, rather than swiping our credit cards at gas pumps and grocery lines, we'll likely zap our payment wirelessly from our phones. Again in Japan, Sony and NTT DoCoMo have teamed up to release a technology enabling cell phones as wireless payment devices. This system, dubbed Felica, uses a RFID (Radio Frequency ID) chip inside the phone to communicate with special readers installed in vending machines or at point-of-purchase in convenience stores.

Meanwhile, your web-enabled phone can already replace your airline boarding pass, helping you avoid not just the hassle of paper tickets and boarding passes, but even the airport kiosk. Instead, your airline emails your boarding pass to your phone, which displays a nice, crisp barcode on the screen. TSA security officers wand your phone, and *voila*, you're on your way. Two test programs, at Continental and AirCanada, are currently doing it.

Oregon's Mount Bachelor ski resort sends opt-in mobile messages to guests with web-enabled phones. The weather and snow reports also feature restaurant coupons or discounts, complete with barcodes that can be scanned by cashiers at Mount Bachelor base lodges.

Ask Mobile GPS gives a glimmer of some of the other possibilities when GPS data and the web meet in a portable device: Get local search results customized to your physical location; share your location with others among your phone contacts or online social networks; display driving directions on your phone.

More Convergence

Mobile isn't the only place witnessing web convergence. The world is getting more digital, more web-enabled, and more portable everywhere you look. Sales of laptops have for the first time outpaced desktop computers. From airports to coffee houses, public libraries to pubs, free WiFi hotspots continue popping up to serve on-the-go laptops and web-enabled mobile devices. Wireless networks are an element of the new public square.

Magellan and the other satellite GPS makers are building wireless internet capabilities into their top-end devices now, and in the future such features will be standard, so that a web-enabled auto navigation unit will access Local Search results, real-time traffic information, local weather forecasts, and more. GM's OnStar system announced a partnership enabling motorists to plan a route online at MapQuest and send it to their car.[18] Once logged into Onstar, they'll get audio turn-by-turn directions.

"One of our goals at MapQuest is to make it convenient and easy for our users to plan their journey on their desktop computers and send the information to their cars," said Jim Greiner, MapQuest general manager.

As I mentioned earlier when discussing local search, phones are natural platforms for voice-activated search. Google Labs has already launched a voice-activated local business directory that can be accessed for free from any phone—just dial 1-800-GOOG-411. While this test application currently connects your phone call to the business, it could (in Google's hands) eventually serve up web search results, product data, stock quotes—any of the specialized results sets currently delivered in response to typed queries.

We're seeing device convergence coming from both sides and poised to meet in the middle: Your phone is web-enabled, while your computer is VOIP-enabled to serve as a phone. Your computer plays full-length movies and music streamed or downloaded from the internet, while your TV and home audio system will be web-enabled to get content from the internet, time-shift your viewing if you so choose, and interact with the programming.

The oft-predicted, slow to arrive "digital home" is making inroads, and will become commonplace. It won't resemble the Jetsons' house and their robotic maid, but will instead consolidate a number of innovations that have been around, in one way or another, for a while. It will be driven by wireless networking of computers and other devices in the home, all linked to the internet. The leading edge is home entertainment, digitized music, movies, and other video programming, streamed or downloaded from the web, networked digital photo frames hanging on the walls, and internet telephony. Other promising web-enabled tools for the home include lighting control and home security, which have the advantage of being monitored and controlled remotely, when a homeowner is traveling, for instance. Subtler forms, like recipe searching from a kitchen laptop or PDA, will become ubiquitous enough to further threaten the print runs of traditional cookbooks. Web-enabled fridges and stoves are on the market, but seem a little farfetched at the moment, offering few discernible advantages over traditional models.

▓ An Internet of Things

One exciting aspect is that innovations are being made simultaneously to so many different but complementary and overlapping networks. GPS technology, satellite, and cellular networks and the internet—whether reached wirelessly or through fiber or satellites—are all working together to a degree. Another fascinating dimension to come is the internetworking of the objects all around us: the "Internet of Things."

In this emerging field, everyday objects will be tagged with Electronic Product Codes or EPCs, discernible through miniature RFID devices, which computers will be able to recognize. Once identified, objects can be tracked and monitored, inventoried, their status used to trigger events like invoicing, package tracking, returns crediting, and more.

RFID technology is already in wide use for things like package scanning and tracking. But broad adoption of EPCs would give business managers a real-time view of physical objects, from widgets to boxcars to blood samples, as they move throughout the global supply chain. That would usher in a revolution in transportation, manufacturing, retail, health care, pharmaceuticals, and countless other fields.

When combined with GPS technology, motion sensors, and the wireless internet, RFID connects the physical world with the internet in truly novel ways. A British firm is developing what it calls the Car2× Communication System so that equipped vehicles can employ sensors and use a wireless LAN network to send and receive information on traffic congestion, accidents, and other problems detected by their onboard sensors, to and from neighboring cars.

Even the humble envelope is getting a Web 3.0 makeover. A winner of the 2007 Red Herring Web2Mobile business plan competition, the Spanish firm IntellaReturn has developed a tiny microchip that can be attached to letters, postcards, and packages to link to text, audio, and video files hosted on the internet. Using a phone or other mobile device equipped with near-field-communication (NFC) equipment, users can then view the multimedia online.[19]

The technology, called Append, works by adding a postage-sized Smart Stamp. "Append keeps traditional mail highly interactive, current and relevant," says the company, "by granting secure 'touch to connect' access for privacy-protected pictures, video, sound, and interactivity—all enabled by the new mobile ecosystem."

Meanwhile, in the same way that today's computers and DVRs routinely hunt across the internet for software upgrades or patches, or for time-sensitive data, in the future we can expect many of our electronic appliances, even our cars, to reach out onto the network and receive alerts, new data, and new software. The web will increasingly serve as the communication channel and instant-delivery network that will keep all our important devices (and many of our unimportant ones!) up-to-date and connected.

Conclusion

In just a few decades, the internet has traveled a wild road, from an obscure Defense Department project to commercial boomtown—and now, with Web 2.0, to a rich and highly social space that is inextricable from the daily life experience of over a billion people worldwide. Some fast-growing and hyped websites of the Web 2.0 era may prove to be mere fads; after kicking the tires for several months, many web users will move on to something else. But while the popularity of particular sites will ebb and flow, and modes of interacting with the web will change with innovations in computer and mobile technology, one thing is certain: The web has become a key gathering place and expression of our culture. The web is arguably more vibrant, fast-moving, and all-inclusive than the offline media that it has in some measure eclipsed. Well, perhaps "supplanted" is too strong a word—"supplemented" is better. After all, this same era saw the renaissance of coffee shop culture.

Web 2.0 has made websites more dynamic, more entertaining, and delivered them anywhere, anytime, over whatever device you carry in your pocket. To succeed in the Web 2.0 world, businesses don't need to invest millions in develop cutting edge technology. What they need to do is embrace the basic, core values that have emerged from the online culture:

- Make your website fun and entertaining to use.
- Let your customers and visitors express themselves, interact with you, and with each other.
- Free your site from the constraints of the PC, offering your data in forms suitable for mobile devices whenever and wherever your customers are.

Appendix A: The Technologies Driving Web 2.0

Glossary

A/B Test: A marketing tool that tests two alternative versions of your homepage, say, or online ad copy, important navigation elements, "landing pages," etc. They track which version delivers the best conversion rate, average order value, or other key metrics. Such tests are performed in real time, with variations served up randomly to segments of your web traffic.

AJAX: "Asynchronous JavaScript and XML." JavaScript is a client-side programming language—it runs in the visitor's browser, not on the server of the website. It's a fast, "lightweight" tool that needn't refresh a whole web page to change what it displays. Paired with XML-formatted data sources, JavaScript can produce fast, dynamic, and interactive web interfaces, where users can click, drag, type, and perform other actions to instantly change a page without waiting for it to reload.

API Web Services: Tool kits that let outside developers reach into their data and re-present it in innovative ways. Also known as APIs (for "Application Programming Interfaces"), these are basically instructions telling outside programmers how to call on their data.

Atom: Like RSS, Atom is an XML language for creation of web data feeds. These feeds let users "subscribe" to have XML formatted data sent to them, rather than having to visit the website that created it.

Behavioral Targeting, or BT, uses cookies to track a web user's past behaviors and predict which advertising he will best respond to.

Bot: As in robot, this is a program that runs repeatedly and automatically— to crawl the web, for instance. (The word Bot can also describe a computer that has been taken over by a web virus—see Chapter 7.)

CAN-SPAM: An acronym for the 2003 Congressional Act, whose full name is, "Controlling the Assault of Non-Solicited Pornography and Marketing Act." In the words of the FTC, it "establishes requirements for those who send commercial email, spells out penalties for spammers and companies whose products are advertised in spam if they violate the law, and gives consumers the right to ask emailers to stop spamming them."

Cloud Computing: Approaching the internet not as a web of separate devices, but as a massive supercomputer. The network of distributed computing power, and of limitless data storage, is the cloud—a resource "out there" that individual users and businesses could harness on demand. Local data storage, and installing expensive software on your own PC or LAN, could become things of the past.

Deep Web: The universe of information that's out of reach of traditional web crawlers. Called the "Invisible Web" or the "Deep Web," it consists of data unknown to the search engines because it is called dynamically from databases by uncrawlable websites, or sealed up in video, audio, and Flash files, and other content types the text-based crawlers can't fully understand. The deep web dwarfs the entire visible web—it's estimated to be some 550 times bigger.

Flash: Lightweight vector-animation tools, like Flash and its new Microsoft cousin Silverlight, energize a website with videos, images, text, and navigation that moves, fades, grows, and responds to user's clicks and mouseovers.

FOAF File: "Friend of a Friend" is a specification for the Semantic Web, which is particularly relevant to programming for social networks. FOAF describes people and the relationships between them.

GUI: Graphical User Interface—your site's navigation design and overall "look and feel."

LAMP: An acronym for four *open-source* software applications that make up a "stack," or bundled combination, used to support websites. LAMP consists of the Linux operating system, Apache servers, MySQL databases, and PHP programming code. As an open-source approach to web applications and hosting, LAMP initially contrasted with proprietary web software such as Microsoft's .NET framework, and Sun's Java-Solaris stack. But nowadays, distinctions are more blurred—Sun has acquired MySQL and embraced the open-source strategy, for instance, and a lot of other proprietary web software can now work with open-source tools.

Link Juice: The search-engine ranking benefit you get when someone else's site links to you (see Page Rank).

Mashup: A program that combines two or more sources of online data to produce something new.

M-Commerce: Online transactions conducted over a PDA, web-enabled cell phone, or other mobile device.

Microsite: A small, purpose-built website with its own look-and-feel and domain name, distinct from its corporate parent site, and aimed at supporting an individual marketing campaign, contest, promotion, brand, product, movie, etc. Microsites are gaining favor as landing pages for online advertising campaigns, and more, because they're often more effective at sharpening a message and cutting through online clutter.

Mobi: The top-level domain for mobile websites, that is, websites designed and formatted for the small screens and keypads of cell phones, PDAs, and other web-enabled mobile devices. There's no consensus whether the .mobi domain-name extension will take off as a convention for hosting mobile websites, or whether site owners will simply employ *user agent sniffing* to identify mobile devices and serve up appropriate mobile content at their main website domain.

MMOGs ("massively multiplayer online games") or MMORPGs ("massively multiplayer online role-playing games"): Online video games like World of Warcraft, Second Life, etc. where players worldwide can interact with each other in a virtual world.

Multivariate Test: These tests display alternative versions of your homepage, say, or important navigation elements or "landing pages," and they track which version—or which combination of several variations—delivers the best conversion rate. Such tests are performed in real-time, with variations served up randomly to segments of your audience.

Open Source: The opposite of "proprietary software" or "licensed software," open source software is available for free. Its underlying source code is also open to modification and improvement, wiki-style, by a community of independent developers. The business model of open-source software companies is to give away the software and make money on premium services like installation, configuration, tech support, training, consulting, etc.

OWL: In the Semantic Web, OWL is the "Web Ontology Language" used to describe the classes and relations between web documents and applications.

Page Rank: The term coined by (and sort of named after) Google founder Larry Page, as a means of ranking the importance of any web page based on the number and quality of other sites linking to that page.

Participatory Web: Describes the characteristic of Web 2.0 in which ordinary users can easily interact with other people online and easily alter and create online content: They can chat online, participate in forums, post comments; share, rate, and review photos and videos; and launch their own blogs, social network profiles, etc.

Podcast: Syndicated online video or audio, usually employing feed technology like RSS or Atom, for playback in a computer or portable media player (like an iPod, hence the name).

Predictive Search: When search engines use stored history to generate suggestions more relevant to each user.

RDF (Resource Description Framework): A markup language for the Semantic Web. Loosely based on XML, it's for describing information and resources on the web, and their relationships to each other.

Realtime Test: The preferred method of website testing, when two versions of your site are delivered simultaneously to two randomly selected segments of your customers. The test quantifies the benefit of a new feature—without introducing any other timing-related variables (like seasonality, marketing mix, product availability) that would muddy the waters.

REST (Representational State Transfer): Transmission of XML data across http. Like SOAP, it's used by web services.

RSS: For "Really Simple Syndication," this technology delivers blog posts and any other content in a highly portable form, so they may be read in a user's personalized homepage or "feed reader" software.

SaaS: "Software as a Service." Software applications that are hosted on the internet and delivered on-demand, through a web browser. SaaS is the Web 2.0 answer to the traditional software model of shrink-wrapped products, installed on a user's PC or local network.

Semantic Web: Coined by Tim Berners-Lee, the Semantic Web is envisioned as a network that is able to describe things in a way that computers can understand, by structuring data into fields and defining the properties of things (like dimensions, prices, age, location) and the relationships between things (one entity is a member of another). The Semantic Web introduced a logical language that human programmers could use to inform computers of the relationships between data—with the goal of replacing the old "web of links" with a new "web of meaning."

Silverlight: Microsoft's answer to Flash, Silverlight is a browser plug-in for delivering rich interactive media and interactive applications for the web.

SOAP (Simple Object Access Protocol): A means for transferring XML-based data across the internet. SOAP is a basic messaging framework used in web services.

Social Advertising: Placing ads on social networking websites. "Social Marketing," covers advertising as well as the online participation, personal outreach, guerilla marketing, and other tactics companies are employing (to mixed effect!) to spread their brands, products, and services in the social media space.

Social Graph: The social graph or social network diagram is, in the words of Brad Fitzpatrick (founder of LiveJournal, chief architect of SixApart, now working at Google) "the global mapping of everybody and how they're related." Social graphs underpin today's social networking sites—they are expressed in, for instance, your "Friend News Feed," and are central to Google's OpenSocial API.

Social Network: Aka social media, any website like Facebook, Myspace, LinkedIn, Friendster, Classmates.com, etc., whose central purpose is to facilitate the connection of individual members. Members establish profiles, create links to a network of friends, and use the site for entertainment, communication, and, well, networking.

Social Search: Applying human wiki and social-networking power to improve search engine results. The new search engines Wikia and Mahalo are the chief examples of this concept.

Social Shopping: Juicing up online shopping with social networking.

Spider: Also known as a "web crawler," this is a program that visits web pages by following the links from one page to another, for the purpose of indexing and (in the case of search engine spiders) ranking them.

Streaming Media: Video and audio files that are transmitted from a web server to the end user. Streaming media basically starts playing a large file immediately without requiring the user to download the entire file before viewing.

Universal Search: Breaking down the walls between content types that previously had lived in their respective silos on specialized search sites: images, videos, news, blogs, maps, and local business listings.

User-Agent Sniffing: For websites, identifying what sort of device a visitor is using—a particular PDA or cell phone, say, versus a desktop or laptop computer—and displaying content designed specifically for that device.

Vertical Search: Or topical search engines, they carve out territory the major engines do poorly. Pixsy and Blinkx index videos, and nothing but videos; Blinkx even uses speech recognition technology to apply text searches to keyword phrases found in videos, audio, and podcasts.

Viral: Growing exponentially, as with hot online news, fads, trends, videos, sites, or marketing campaigns—where each person touched spreads the word to more than one other person. In pre-internet days, most marketing investments produced linear growth. But with the frictionless ease of email and hyperlinking, consumers on the web spread word-of-mouth at an exponential rate. Needless to say, successful computer viruses also chart a viral growth pattern.

Vlog: Video-log, an online video-diary. Powered by the author's cam, it's the Web 2.0 answer to a plain old blog.

WAP: Wireless Application Protocol, an open standard for wireless applications, used by cell phones and other mobile devices to access the web.

Web of Things: The concept of embedding RFID chips into physical objects like packages, cars, etc. so that their status, whereabouts, and other data become part of the internet's current "web of documents."

Web Service: Any software system designed to support interoperable machine-to-machine interaction across the Web.

Widgets: Small, freestanding programs—pieces of HTML and programming code—that can be pasted into any web page. They use JavaScript, DHTML, Flash, or other language to carry out some dynamic action. Web visitor counters, mini-games, clocks, calendars, horoscopes, weather forecasts, and stock tickers are all examples of common widget applications. They may also be called "snippets" or "plug-ins," and Google likes to call them "gadgets."

Wiki: Meaning "quick" in Hawaiian, it is an approach to online collaboration made most famous by Wikipedia, the user-created and edited web encyclopedia. Aka "crowdsourcing" or "distributed workforce."

WOM: Word of mouth. In the web era, also known as "word of mouse."

WML: Wireless Markup Language—the format of websites meant to be viewed by WAP mobile devices.

X3D—An open standard for developing 3-D objects, virtual reality, and "Virtual Worlds" online.

XML: Extensible Markup Language—a formatting language that breaks data into fields and puts it into a form that can be used, manipulated, and represented anywhere on the web.

Appendix B: Web 2.0 Reading and Resource List

Conferences & Events

New Web 2.0-oriented conferences are popping up like mushrooms after rain. And many of the traditional marketing and media conferences now offer 2.0 tracks. Here is a sampling of some of the higher profile, marketing and strategy related shows:

DMA, Direct Marketing Association Conference & Exhibition, http://www.the-dma.org/conferences.
A general-interest direct marketing conference with strong Web 2.0 tracks.

Future of Mobile, http://future-of-mobile.com
London event for "thinkers and practitioners in the mobile industry."

GEL Conference: Good Experience Live, http://www.gelconference.com.
Not strictly a Web 2.0 conference, GEL is dedicated to "exploring good experience in all its forms—in business, technology, art, society, and life." Founder Mark Hurst has captured a zeitgeist, and attracted a community

that is very Web 2.0; attendees are a diverse bunch, but include many from leading web companies.

Internet Retailer Conference & Exposition, http://www.internetretailer.com
A leading internet retailing conference, IRCE brings together a huge swath of online merchants and industry experts, and dedicates a lot of programming to Web 2.0 topics.

Mobile Content Strategies, http://www.mobilecontentstrategies.com/
Addresses the business of supplying content for mobile devices.

Mobile Internet World, http://www.mobilenetx.com
A European conference series recently crossed the Atlantic for an event in Boston. It covers business strategy, emerging technologies and best practices for targeting the mobile internet.

NewTeeVee, http://live.newteevee.com
A new conference targeting the online video and entertainment industry.

SaaScon, http://www.saascon.com/
ComputerWorld-sponsored conferences on software-as-a-service, web services, and cloud computing.

Search Engine Strategies, http://www.searchenginestrategies.com/
A U.S. and international conference series dedicated to paid search advertising and search-engine optimization — including Web 2.0 and mobile topics.

Shop.org, http://www.shop.org
Trade group and conference and seminar sponsor for online retailers.

SMX: Search Marketing Expo, http://searchmarketingexpo.com/
The new search-engine marketing and SEO conference series led by a leading voice in the field, Danny Sullivan.

SXSW: South by Southwest Interactive Festival, http://www.sxsw.com
Part of a larger music and arts event, the interactive festival "Celebrates the creativity and passion behind the coolest new media technologies."

SYS-CON Events, http://events.sys-con.com/
For Web 2.0 developers and CIOs, Sys-Con hosts several events including Ajax World, SOA World, Virtualization Expo, iPhone Developer Summit, and more.

Virtual Worlds Conference & Expo, http://www.virtualworlds2008.com/
Conference series devoted to MMOGs and online Virtual Worlds.

VoiceCon, http://www.voicecon.com/
Conference series devoted to voice communications across the internet: IP telephony, Unified Communications platforms, and "converged networks."

Web 2.0 Expo, http://www.web2expo.com/
The newer and less expensive "companion event" to the Web 2.0 Summit, this US and international conference series is intended for a broader audience—not just the A-players offered an invitation to the Summit.

Web 2.0 Summit, http://www.web2summit.com/
The exclusive, cutting-edge, invitation-only event launched and moderated by John Battelle and Tim O'Reilly, the guys who coined the term "Web 2.0."

▨ Blogs & Websites

John Battelle's Searchblog, http://www.battellemedia.com
Thoughts on the intersection of search, media, technology, and more.

Matt Cutts: Gadgets, Google and SEO, http://www.mattcutts.com/blog/
You really wish you had a connection to a top insider at Google, and could hear what's going on there and why. Matt Cutts is probably as close as you're gonna get.

O'Reilly Media, http://www.oreilly.com.
Books, online training, blog posts and more—dedicated mostly to the technologies, trends and programming languages that power the web.

Programmable Web, http://www.programmableweb.com/
Keeping you up to date with mashups, APIs and the Web as platform.

Read/Write Web, http://www.readwriteweb.com/
Web Apps, web technology trends, social networking and social media.

Seth Godin, http://www.sethgodin.typepad.com
Daily, and dependably brilliant, marketing insights.

TechCrunch, http://www.techcrunch.com/
A blog captained by Michael Arrington and Erick Schonfeld, covering the latest Internet technology, gossip, buyouts, and Web 2.0 business stories.

Technorati, http://www.technorati.com
The authority on blogs, online news, and social bookmarks. When last we looked, Technorati was tracking 112.8 million blogs and over 250 million pieces of tagged social media.

Valleywag, http://valleywag.com/
Tabloid-style news and gossip about Silicon Valley.

Web 2.0 Journal, http://www.web2journal.com/
News and print publications dedicated to Web 2.0 technology, development and other topics.

Web 2.0 Work Group, http://www.web20workgroup.com
A network of blogs devoted to Web 2.0 topics, including Techcrunch, Read/WriteWeb and WeBreakStuff.

▒ Magazines

Business 2.0, http://money.cnn.com/magazines/business2/

DM News, http://www.dmnews.com/

Internet Retailer, http://www.internetretailer.com/

Multichannel Merchant, http://multichannelmerchant.com/

Revenue, http://www.revenuetoday.com/

Wired, http://www.wired.com/

▒ Books

Anderson, Chris. *The Long Tail: Why the Future of Business is Selling Less of More*. New York: Hyperion, 2006.
Battelle, John. *The Search: How Google and its Rivals Rewrote the Rules of Business and Transformed Our Culture*. New York: Penguin, 2005.
Carr, Nicholas. *The Big Switch: Rewiring the World, from Edison to Google*. New York: W.W. Norton, 2008.
Fensel, Dieter, et al., Foreword by Tim Berners-Lee. *Spinning the Semantic Web: Bringing the World Wide Web to Its Full Potential*. Cambridge: MIT Press, 2003.
Freedman, Lauren. *It's Just Shopping: eMerchant meets eShopper*. New York: Direct Marketing Association, 2002.
Gillin, Paul. *The New Influencers: A Marketer's Guide to the New Social Media*. Sanger, CA: Quill Driver Books, 2007.
Gladwell, Malcolm. *The Tipping Point: How Little Things Can Make a Big Difference*. New York: Little, Brown, 2002.
Godin, Seth. *Meatball Sundae: Is Your Marketing out of Sync?* New York: Penguin, 2007.
———. *Permission Marketing: Turning Strangers Into Friends And Friends Into Customers*. New York: Simon & Schuster, 1999.
———. *Unleashing the Ideavirus*. New York: Hyperion, 2001.

McConnell, Ben & Huba, Jackie. *Citizen Marketers: When People Are the Message.* New York: Kaplan Publishing, 2006.

Tapscott, Don & Williams, Anthony. *Wikinomics: How Mass Collaboration Changes Everything.* New York: Penguin, 2006.

Weber, Larry. *Marketing to the Social Web: How Digital Customer Communities Build Your Business.* San Francisco: John Wiley & Sons, 2007.

Notes

Introduction: What is Web 2.0 and How Will It Change My Business?

1. Tim O'Reilly, "What Is Web 2.0?" September 30, 2005, O'Reilly Media Inc., http://www.oreilly.com/pub/a/orielly/tim/news/2005/09/30/what-is-web.html.

2. John Pallatto, "Web 2.0 Lacks Meaning, Magic," *eWeek*, December 27, 2005, http://www.eweek.com/article2/0,1759,1906053,00.asp.

1. Power to the People

1. Adam Sarner, et al., "Gartner's Top Predictions for IT Organizations and Users, 2007 and Beyond," Gartner Research, December 1, 2006.

2. Dave Sifry, "The State of the Live Web, April 2007," Technorati, http://www.technorati.com/weblog/2007/04/328.html.

3. "Social Network Pumps up Average Order and Conversion," November 13, 2007, Internet Retailer, http://www.internetretailer.com/dailyNews.asp?id=24394.

4. Joel Stein, "The Accidental 'Friend' Finder," *Business 2.0*, April 2007.

5. Jimmy Wales, remarks made during "Craig Newmark Keynote Interview," South by Southwest Conference, Austin, TX, March 13, 2006.

6. Seth Godin, email interview with the author. Godin tells the BlendTec story in detail in *Meatball Sundae: Is Your Marketing Out of Sync?* New York: Penguin, 2007.

7. "Top Search Terms Reveal Web Users Rely on Search Engines to Navigate Their Way to Common Sites," Nielsen/NetRatings Report, January 18, 2006.

8. Amanda Lenhart, et al., "Teens and Social Media," *Pew Internet & American Life Project*, December 19, 2007, http://www.pewinternet.org/PPF/r/230/report_display. asp.

2. Pull Media, Not Push

1. Eileen Alt Powell, Associated Press, January 10, 2008, http://i.abcnews.com/ Business/IndustryInfo/wireStory?id=4113845.

2. "Annual Spam Report," December 12, 2007, Barracuda Networks, http://www. barracudanetworks.com/ns/news_and_events/index.php?nid=232.

3. "Search Engine Users' Attitudes," *iProspect & Survey Sample International*, May 5, 2004.

4. "The 2007 Email Marketing Survey: Looking Forward," *Datran Media Research*, December 2006.

5. "comScore Widget Metrix," comScore Media Metrix, June 2007, http://www. comscore.com/press/release.asp?press=1471.

6. Barry Parr, et al., "Widgets: Delivering Applications Users Want," *JupiterResearch*, November 16, 2007.

7. "Advertising Widgets Help Site Publishers Reap Cash," *Internet Retailer*, November 12, 2007, http://www.internetretailer.com/internet/marketing-conference/666373064-advertising-widgets-help-site-publishers-reap-cash.html.

8. "A Glimpse of the Next Episode," *Nokia & The Future Laboratory*, December 3, 2007.

9. Scene 7 Lenox Case Study, May 2, 2006, http://www.scene7.com/clients/ lenox2.asp.

3. The Web as Platform: The Network Is the Computer

1. "2007 Survey of Viewer Trends in TV and Online Video," ChoiceStream, December 2007, http://www.choicestream.com/videosurveyresults/ ChoiceStream_Survey-ViewerTrends-TV_OnlineVideo2007.pdf.

2. "Going Mobile: An International Study of Content Use and Advertising on the Mobile Web," Online Publishers Association, March 2007.

3. "Mobile Phone Web Users Nearly Equal PC-Based Internet Users in Japan," comScore Media Metrix, September 20, 2007, http://www.comscore.com/press/ release.asp?press=1742.

4. Antony Bruno, "iPhone Spurs Web Traffic, If Not Music Sales," Reuters, January 18, 2008; and Miguel Helft, "Google Sees Surge in iPhone Traffic," *New York Times*, January 14, 2008.

5. "Mobile Web Sites: Designing for Mobility," *JupiterResearch*, January 2008.

4. Case Studies: Rapidly Changing Online Landscapes

1. Steve Ballmer, keynote address, Association of National Advertisers Annual Conference, Phoenix, AZ, October 11, 2007.

2. James Montgomery and Gil Kaufman, "The Year the Music Industry Broke," MTV News, December 17, 2007, http://www.mtv.com/news/articles/1576538/20071214/madonna.jhtml.

3. "Broadband Content and Services 2007," *Horowitz Associates*, December 4, 2007.

4. Lee Rainie, "Pew Internet Project Data Memo," Pew Internet & American Life Project, January 9, 2008, http://www.pewinternet.org/pdfs/Pew_Videosharing_memo_Jan08.pdf.

5. Jack Plunkett: Plunkett Research, Ltd., http://www.plunkettresearch.com.

6. "Young Adults Show Significant Interest in Free Ad-Supported TV Show Downloads," Ipsos Insight, January 8, 2008, http://www.ipsosinsight.com/act_dsp_view_pdf.aspx?name=mr080108-1rev3.pdf&id=3781.

7. Netflix CEO, Reed Hastings, Q1 Financial Results Analysts' Conference Call, April 18, 2007.

8. Martin Olausson, "Games Industry Transformed As One-Third of Games Software Revenues Will Be Generated Online by 2011," Strategy Analytics, September 10, 2007, http://www.strategyanalytics.net/default.aspx?mod=PressReleaseViewer&a0=3569.

9. Seth Schiesel, "The Video Game May Be Free, But to Be a Winner Can Cost Money," *The New York Times*, January 21, 2008.

10. "Active Gamer Benchmark Study," *Nielsen Entertainment*, October 5, 2006.

11. "Rocketing Internet Advertising to Overtake Radio," ZenithOptimedia global advertising report, December 2007, http://www.zenithoptimedia.com/gff/pdf/Advertising%20Expenditure%20Forecasts%20%20March%202007.pdf.

12. "DoubleClick Performics 50 Search Trend Report Q1 2007," DoubleClick Performics, June 2007, http://www.doubleclick.com/insight/downloadResearch.aspx?fileName=DoubleclickPerformics50_Q1_2007.pdf.

13. "Giving Clicks Credit Where They're Due: What You Need to Know When Allocating Your Search Budget," 360i and SearchIgnite, December 2006, http://www.360i.com/brandwhitepaper/whitepaper-web.pdf.

14. "Social Network Marketing: Ad Spending and Usage," eMarketer, December 2007, http://www.emarketer.com/Reports/All/Emarketer_2000478.aspx?src=report_head_info_reports.

15. Ibid.

16. "Behavioral Advertising on Target...to Explode Online," eMarketer, June 2007, http://www.emarketer.com/Article.aspx?id=1004989.

17. "Online Video Content: The New TV Audience," eMarketer, February 2007, http://www.emarketer.com/Reports/All/Emarketer_2000454.aspx?src= report_head_info_reports.

18. "Consumers Shout 'I Want My Online Video,'" *Online Insights*, Burst Media, December 2007, http://www.burstmedia.com/assets/newsletter/items/2008_01_01.pdf.

19. Harold Stringer, remarks made at the World Economic Forum, Davos, Switzerland, January 23–27, 2008, reported in *The Financial Times*, http://www.ft.com/cms/s/0/e7c50fce-ced6-11dc-877a-000077b07658.html?nclick_check=1.

20. Tateru Nino, "Mixed Reality Headcount: Top 10 Corporate Sites in Second Life," New World Notes, blog post on November 12, 2007, http://nwn.blogs.com/nwn/mixed_reality_headcount/index.html.

21. Joey Seiler, "Virtual Worlds Management Industry Forecast 2008," Virtual Worlds News, December 17, 2007, http://www.virtualworldsnews.com/2007/12/this-virtual-wo.html.

22. Julie Ask, et al., "Mobile Web Sites: Designing for Mobility," *JupiterResearch*, January 11, 2008.

23. John du Pre Gauntt, "Mobile Search: Clash of the Titans," eMarketer, July 24, 2007, http://www.emarketer.com/Article.aspx?id=1005170&src=article1_newsltr.

24. Lauren Freedman, interview with the author.

25. "eHoliday Survey," *Shop.org & BizRate*, October 24, 2007.

26. "Top 100 Online Retail Satisfaction Index," *ForeSee Results*, May 2007.

27. "Holiday Sales Expectations," Internet Retailer/Vovici, November 2007, http://www.internetretailer.com/article.asp?id=24246.

28. "The 2006 Transformed Multi-Channel Shopper," the e-tailing group and J.C. Williams Group, July 2006, http://www.e-tailing.com/research/multi_channel/press/MCTransformation724final.pdf.

29. "Search Engine Claims the Human Touch," IT News, June 5, 2007, http://www.itnews.com.au/News/NewsStory.aspx?story=53514.

30. Jack Menzel, Google, remarks made at the Search Engine Strategies Conference, New York, March 19, 2008.

5. Successful Online Business Models for Web 2.0 and Beyond

1. Google, Quarterly Financial Results, February 1, 2008.

2. Scott Scheleur, et al., "Quarterly Retail e-Commerce Sales, 2nd Quarter 2007," Census Bureau, United States Commerce Department, August 16, 2007.

3. "MegaView Online Retail," Nielsen NetRatings, reported in *Internet Retailer*, January 29, 2008, http://www.internetretailer.com/dailyNews.asp?id=25187.

4. Kevin Hillstrom, remarks made at NEMOA (New England Mail Order Association), Spring 2007 Conference, Cambridge, MA, March 21, 2007.

5. Safa Rashtchy, remarks made at "The Wall Street View of eCommerce and Multichannel Retailing," 2006 *Shop.org* Annual Summit, October 12, 2006.

6. Alan Rimm Kauffman, "Quack, Quack: Made-For-AdSense Spam," post to Rimm-Kauffman Group blog, January 25, 2008, http://www.rimmkaufman.com/rkgblog/2008/01/25/mfa-duck/.

7. Stewart Brand, remarks made at the first Annual Hackers Conference, Marin, CA, November 1984.

8. Erick Schonfeld, "CNN.com Comes to Its Senses, Abandons Pipeline," posting on Business 2.0's blog, May 23, 2007, archived at http://nextnet.typepad.com/the_next_net/2007/05/cnncom-comes-to.html.

9. Frank Ahrens, "Web Sites Tear Down That Wall," *The Washington Post*, November 17, 2007.

10. Matt Richtel, "For Pornographers, Internet's Virtues Turn to Vices," *The New York Times*, June 2, 2007.

11. "Online Nation: Five Years of Growth in Online Learning," Sloan Consortium, November 2007, http://www.sloan-c.org/publications/survey/pdf/online_nation.pdf.

12. "No Future for Paid Video Downloads," Forrester Research, May 14, 2007, http://www.forrester.com/ER/Press/Release/0,1769,1144,00.html.

13. Anne Holland, Marketing Sherpa, remarks made at the keynote address, Affiliate Summit 2006, West, Las Vegas, NV, January 8, 2006.

6. Ten Things You Should Do to Make Your Business More "Web 2.0"

1. Marc Andreessen, remarks made at the Web 2.0 Summit, San Francisco, CA, November 8, 2006.

2. Tom Kothmann, remarks made at 2008 ACCM Conference, Orlando, FL, May 21, 2008.

3. "Social Shopping Study," the e-tailing group and *Power Reviews*, November 2007.

4. Seth Godin, email interview with the author.

5. Patti Freeman Evans, "Retail Marketing: Driving Sales through Consumer-Created Content," *JupiterResearch*, August 2006.

6. "Customer Ratings Tested," *Marketing Experiments Journal*, November 29, 2004, http://www.marketingexperiments.com/improving-website-conversion/customer-ratings.html.

7. No Fish Story: Customer Reviews Reel in Higher Sales at BassPro.com," *Internet Retailer*, September 27, 2006.

8. Matt Hawkins, "Social Navigation Drives Sales at PETCO.com," Bazaarvoice case study, September 6, 2007, http://www.bazaarvoice.com/cs_rr_sort_Petco.html.

9. Matt Hawkins, "Social Navigation Drives Sales at PETCO.com," Bazaarvoice case study, September 6, 2007, http://www.bazaarvoice.com/cs_rr_sort_Petco.html.

10. "Security Concerns Are Causing Shoppers to Limit Spending Online," *Ipsos-Insight*, January 2004.

11. "Marketing & Media Survey," *Datran Media*, January 22, 2008.

12. "The Power of Direct Marketing," Direct Marketing Association, August 2006.

13. David Daniels, "The ROI of Email Relevance: Improving Campaign Results through Targeting," *JupiterResearch*, May 25, 2005.

14. Ken Kikkawa, email interview with the author.

15. Bill Nussey, remarks at Silverpop Digital Marketer Conference, Atlanta, GA, May 3, 2006

16. Ken Kikkawa, email interview with the author.

17. Barry Chu, remarks at Search Engine Strategies Conference, New York, March 19, 2008.

18. Brian Quinton, "Young But Not Stupid," *Promo Magazine*, February 2008.

7. The Dark Side: How the Latest Developments in Cyber Crime Can Ruin Your Day—Or Business

1. "2008 Online Fraud Report," *CyberSource*, January 2008.

2. "Microsoft Security Intelligence Report (January–June 2007)," Microsoft, http://www.microsoft.com/sir.

3. Anne Holland, Marketing Sherpa, remarks at keynote address, Affiliate Summit 2006 West, Las Vegas, NV, January 8, 2006.

4. Attila Balazs, virus researcher, "Trojan.Qhost.WU," BitDefender, December 17, 2007, http://www.bitdefender.com/VIRUS-1000239-en−Trojan.Qhost.WU.html.

5. Niels Provos, et al., "The Ghost in the Browser: Analysis of Web-Based Malware," Google, Inc., 2007.

6. Alex Eckelberry, "Massive Amounts of Malware Redirects in Searches," post to Sunbelt Software blog, November 26, 2007, http://sunbeltblog.blogspot.com/2007/11/breaking-massive-amounts-of-malware.html.

7. Betsy Schiffman, "Rogue Anti-Virus Slimeballs Hide Malware in Ads," posted on *Wired* Blog Network, November 15, 2007, http://blog.wired.com/business/2007/11/doubleclick-red.html.

8. "New Attacks That Exploit Widgets and Gadgets Are Imminent," Finjan Security, September 17, 2007, http://www.finjan.com/Pressrelease.aspx?id=1705.

9. "Facebook Widget Installing Spyware," Fortinet, January 2, 2008, http://www.fortiguardcenter.com/advisory/FGA-2007-16.html. Details of Zango's unrelated FTC suit can be found at "Zango Inc. Settles FTC Charges," Federal Trade Commission, November 3, 2006, http://www.ftc.gov/opa/2006/11/zango.shtm.

10. John Pescatore and John Girard, "Fast-Spreading Virus or Worm Won't Affect Mobile Devices Before Year-End 2007," *Gartner Research*, June 10, 2005.

11. "Worldwide Mobile Phone 2007–2011 Forecast Update," *IDC*, December 2007.

12. Tom Espiner, "Researchers Hack Microsoft Wireless Keyboards," CNET News.com, December 5, 2007, http://www.news.com/Researchers-hack-Microsoft-wireless-keyboards/2100-7347_3-6221593.html.

8. Web 3.0: What Does the Future Hold?

1. Tim-Berners Lee, remarks at the 15th Annual International World Wide Web Conference, Edinburgh, Scotland, reported by Victoria Shannon, *International Herald Tribune*, May 24, 2006.

2. Reed Hastings, remarks to Technet Summit, Palo Alto, CA, November 15, 2006.

3. Jerry Yang, remarks at Technet Summit, Palo Alto, CA, November 15, 2006.

4. Jason Calacanis, "Web 3.0, the 'Official' Definition," blog post October 3, 2007, http://www.calacanis.com/2007/10/03/web-3-0-the-official-definition/.

5. Eric Schmidt, remarks at the Seoul Digital Forum, Seoul, South Korea, March 8, 2008, http://www.youtube.com/watch?v=T0QJmmdw3b0.

6. Tim Berners-Lee, "What the Semantic Web Is Not," World Wide Web Consortium, September 1998, http://www.w3.org/DesignIssues/RDFnot.html.

7. Tim Berners-Lee, *Weaving the Web*, San Francisco: HarperOne, 1999.

8. Alex Iskold, "Web 3.0: When Web Sites Become Web Services," posted March 19, 2007, http://www.readwriteweb.com/archives/web_30_when_web_sites_become_web_services.php.

9. "IBM Introduces Ready-to-Use Cloud Computing," IBM, November 15, 2007, http://www-03.ibm.com/press/us/en/pressrelease/22613.wss.

10. "Yahoo! Launches New Program to Advance Open-Source Software for Internet Computing," Yahoo!, November 12, 2007, http://yahoo.client.shareholder.com/press/releasedetail.cfm?ReleaseID=275236.

11. "IBM and Linden Lab Launch Collaboration to Further Advance the 3-D Internet," October 10, 2007, http://www-03.ibm.com/press/us/en/pressrelease/22428.wss.

12. "iMeme: The Thinkers of Tech," *Fortune*, July 2007.

13. Frank Moss, remarks at "Virtual Worlds: Where Business, Society, Technology & Policy Converge," MIT Media Lab Conference, Cambridge, MA, June 15, 2007.

14. Barbara Ortutay, "Mind Control? Gaming Headset Will Do Just That," MSNBC/Associated Press, February 20, 2008, http://www.msnbc.msn.com/id/23261794/.

15. "Paralyzed Man Takes a Walk in Virtual World," Agence France-Presse, June 2, 2008.

16. Eric Schmidt, remarks at 2008 World Economic Forum, Davos, Switzerland, January 25, 2008.

17. John Battelle, "The Transparent (Shopping) Society," posted November 9, 2004, http://battellemedia.com/archives/001023.php.

18. "OnStar Expands its Navigation Service with MapQuest Partnership," April 25, 2007, http://www.onstar.com/us_english/jsp/new_at_onstar/mapquest.jsp.

19. Ryan Olson, "Web-2-Mobile Picks Winners," *Red Herring*, January 24, 2007, http://www.redherring.com/Home/20956.

Index

About the Author

TOM FUNK has been involved in ecommerce and Web publishing since 1995. In his six years managing the websites of the Vermont Teddy Bear Company, Funk saw online revenues triple, and the company's sites were named to Internet Retailer's "Best of the Web" Top 50. Funk is currently VP of Client Services for Timberline Interactive, a Web development and online marketing consultancy.